D0776888

THIS JOURNAL
BELONGS TO:

...........................
...........................
...........................

# THE
# ME
# J☼URNAL

## Shane Windham

*"Tend to your dreams; you may harvest them all."*
—SHANE WINDHAM

You can keep this volume as a private journal
to chronicle your own unique stories, thoughts,
opinions, likes and dislikes, hopes and dreams;
or share it with close friends and family. With
over 300 pages to fill out, in the end you will
have recorded the story of you.

**STERLING**
New York

An Imprint of Sterling Publishing
1166 Avenue of the Americas
New York, NY 10036

ISBN 978-1-4549-1933-9

Distributed in Canada by Sterling Publishing
c/o Canadian Manda Group, 664 Annette Street
Toronto, Ontario, Canada M6S 2C8
Distributed in the United Kingdom by GMC Distribution Services
Castle Place, 166 High Street, Lewes, East Sussex, England BN7 1XU
Distributed in Australia by Capricorn Link (Australia) Pty. Ltd.
P.O. Box 704, Windsor, NSW 2756, Australia

For information about custom editions, special sales, and premium
and corporate purchases, please contact Sterling Special Sales at
800-805-5489 or specialsales@sterlingpublishing.com.

Manufactured in China

8  10  9  7

www.sterlingpublishing.com

## MUSIC FAVORITES

ARTIST NAME: _____

ALBUM: _____

SONG/LYRIC: _____

_____

What or who do these lyrics remind you of?

_____

_____

ARTIST NAME: _____

ALBUM: _____

SONG/LYRIC: _____

_____

What or who do these lyrics remind you of?

_____

_____

ARTIST NAME: _____

ALBUM: _____

SONG/LYRIC: _____

_____

What or who do these lyrics remind you of?

_____

_____

"Knowing yourself is the beginning of all wisdom."

—Aristotle

Right now I am thinking . . .

# YOUR LISTS

Your favorite apps:

1. _____
2. _____
3. _____
4. _____
5. _____
6. _____
7. _____
8. _____

Your favorite herbs:

1. _____
2. _____
3. _____
4. _____
5. _____
6. _____
7. _____
8. _____

# YOUR LISTS

Actors you like:

1. _____

2. _____

3. _____

Actors you dislike:

1. _____

2. _____

3. _____

Actresses you like:

1. _____

2. _____

3. _____

Actresses you dislike:

1. _____

2. _____

3. _____

# YOUR LEAST FAVORITE

Age:

_____

Curse word:

_____

Day of the week:

_____

Exercise:

_____

Liquor:

_____

Mode of travel:

_____

Month of the year:

_____

Piece of clothing:

_____

Planet:

_____

Season:

_____

Sport:

_____

# YOUR MOST FAVORITE

Age:

Curse word:

Day of the week:

Exercise:

Liquor:

Mode of travel:

Month of the year:

Piece of clothing:

Planet:

Season:

Sport:

# WHAT ARE YOUR THOUGHTS ON . . . ?

Cryogenics?

_____

_____

_____

_____

Hitchhikers?

_____

_____

_____

_____

Gluten?

_____

_____

_____

_____

Equality?

_____

_____

_____

_____

## THIS OR THAT
(CIRCLE YOUR PREFERENCE)

Horns OR Strings

Looks OR Functionality

Sequels OR Prequels

Quotes OR Memes

Lead OR Follow

Past OR Future

Save money OR Save time

Curly hair OR Straight hair

Shooting pool OR Playing catch

Boots OR Sneakers

Instrumental OR Vocals

Swimming OR Skiing

Flannel OR Wool

T-shirts OR Button downs

Cup half empty OR Cup half full

Trains OR Planes

E-books OR Physical books

Religious OR Spiritual

Jump out of bed OR Wake up slowly

Well done OR Rare

Tight clothing OR Loose clothing

Intuition OR Facts

Back seat OR Front seat

Museums OR Historical landmarks

Daytime walks OR Nighttime walks

Gym workouts OR Outdoor workouts

City sidewalks OR Mountain trails

# TELEVISION FAVORITES

SHOW TITLE: _____

EPISODE/SEASON: _____

What did you like about this show?

_____

_____


SHOW TITLE: _____

EPISODE/SEASON: _____

What did you like about this show?

_____

_____


SHOW TITLE: _____

EPISODE/SEASON: _____

What did you like about this show?

_____

_____


SHOW TITLE: _____

EPISODE/SEASON: _____

What did you like about this show?

_____

_____

SHOW TITLE: _____

EPISODE/SEASON: _____

What did you like about this show?

_____

_____


SHOW TITLE: _____

EPISODE/SEASON: _____

What did you like about this show?

_____

_____


SHOW TITLE: _____

EPISODE/SEASON: _____

What did you like about this show?

_____

_____


SHOW TITLE: _____

EPISODE/SEASON: _____

What did you like about this show?

_____

_____

# YOUR LISTS

Your favorite things to dream about:

1. _____
2. _____
3. _____
4. _____
5. _____
6. _____
7. _____
8. _____

Your least favorite things to dream about:

1. _____
2. _____
3. _____
4. _____
5. _____
6. _____
7. _____
8. _____

Vegetables you like:

1. _____
2. _____
3. _____
4. _____
5. _____
6. _____
7. _____
8. _____

Vegetables you dislike:

1. _____
2. _____
3. _____
4. _____
5. _____
6. _____
7. _____
8. _____

"Have patience with everything that remains unsolved in your heart."

—RAINER MARIA RILKE,
*Letters to a Young Poet*

I am inspired by . . .

## WHEN SOMEONE SAYS _____,
## YOU THINK . . .

Adventure:

_____

Airplanes:

_____

Animation:

_____

Annoying:

_____

Babies:

_____

Balloons:

_____

Bandages:

_____

Beard:

_____

Bees:

_____

Bells:

_____

Bicycle:

_____

# AT RANDOM

Have you taken an IQ test?
[✓] yes  [ ] no

Pizza toppings you like:

____ Anchovies          ✓ Olives
____ Artichokes         ✓ Onions
✓ Bacon                 ✓ Peppers
____ Basil              ✓ Pepperoni
____ Broccoli           ____ Pineapple
✓ Canadian bacon        ✓ Sausage
✓ Chicken               ____ Spinach
____ Mushrooms          ____ Sun-dried tomatoes

One bad thing you think an ex might have to say about you:

_____

One good thing you think an ex might have to say about you:

_____

Do clowns scare you?
[✓] yes  [ ] no

How many times have you been in love? ____

Do you like to dance?
[ ] yes  [✓] no

                    Can you carry a tune?
                    [✓] yes  [ ] no

# YOUR LEAST FAVORITE

Author:
_____

Card game:
_____

Cookie:
_____

Color combination:
_____

Insect:
_____

Olympic event:
_____

Place to be alone:
_____

Street in your town:
_____

Subject in school:
_____

Time of day:
_____

Type of food:
_____

# YOUR MOST FAVORITE

Author:

_____

Card game:

_____

Cookie:

_____

Color combination:

_____

Insect:

_____

Olympic event:

_____

Place to be alone:

_____

Street in your town:

_____

Subject in school:

_____

Time of day:

_____

Type of food:

_____

# YOUR LISTS

Your four greatest phobias:

1. _____
2. _____
3. _____
4. _____
5. _____

Names you'd give a child:

1. _____
2. _____
3. _____
4. _____
5. _____

Languages you'd love to be able to speak:

1. _____
2. _____
3. _____
4. _____
5. _____

Things your family taught you to appreciate:

1. _____
2. _____
3. _____
4. _____
5. _____
6. _____

The biggest celebrities you've met or seen out and about:

1. _____
2. _____
3. _____
4. _____
5. _____
6. _____

Your most memorable Halloween costumes:

1. _____
2. _____
3. _____
4. _____
5. _____
6. _____

Strange food combinations you like:

1. _____
2. _____
3. _____
4. _____
5. _____
6. _____
7. _____
8. _____
9. _____
10. _____

Foods that do not go well together:

1. _____
2. _____
3. _____
4. _____
5. _____
6. _____
7. _____
8. _____
9. _____
10. _____

## TODAY I . . . READ:

(LIST ALL OF THE THINGS YOU READ TODAY—
NEWSPAPERS, MAGAZINES, BOOKS, BLOGS, REVIEWS,
WORK- OR SCHOOL-RELATED TEXTS)

DATE: _____

1. _____

2. _____

3. _____

4. _____

5. _____

6. _____

7. _____

8. _____

9. _____

10. _____

11. _____

12. _____

13. _____

14. _____

15. _____

16. _____

# WHAT ARE YOUR THOUGHTS ON . . . ?

Alternative medicine?

_____

_____

_____

_____

Electronic voice phenomenon?

_____

_____

_____

_____

The economy and the job market?

_____

_____

_____

_____

Music sampling?

_____

_____

_____

_____

# AT RANDOM

Things you've been known to do in your sleep:

| | |
|---|---|
| ____ Drool | ____ Scream |
| ____ Hit | ____ Sing |
| ____ Kick | ____ Smile |
| ____ Laugh | ____ Snore |
| ____ Open your eyes | ____ Talk |

Types of homes you've lived in:

| | |
|---|---|
| ____ Apartment/Condo | ✓ House |
| ____ Boat | ____ Loft |
| ____ Cabin | ____ Mobile home |
| ____ Car/RV | ____ Tent |

You have the biggest issues with which one of the following:

| | |
|---|---|
| ____ Allergies | ✓ Headaches |
| ____ Constipation | ____ Indigestion |
| ____ Diarrhea | ✓ Muscle aches |
| ____ Gas | ____ Rashes |

Art forms you've tried your hand at:

| | |
|---|---|
| ____ Acting | ✓ Painting |
| ____ Architecture | ✓ Photography |
| ✓ Crafts | ____ Sculpting |
| ____ Culinary | ____ Sewing |
| ____ Dance | ✓ Singing |
| ✓ Drawing | ✓ Video |
| ____ Landscaping | ____ Woodworking |
| ✓ Music | ✓ Writing |

# FILM FAVORITES

FILM NAME: _____

FAVORITE CHARACTER: _____

WHERE DID YOU SEE IT? _____

WHO DID YOU SEE IT WITH? _____

What did you like about this film?

_____


FILM NAME: _____

FAVORITE CHARACTER: _____

WHERE DID YOU SEE IT? _____

WHO DID YOU SEE IT WITH? _____

What did you like about this film?

_____


FILM NAME: _____

FAVORITE CHARACTER: _____

WHERE DID YOU SEE IT? _____

WHO DID YOU SEE IT WITH? _____

What did you like about this film?

_____

FILM NAME: _____

FAVORITE CHARACTER: _____

WHERE DID YOU SEE IT? _____

WHO DID YOU SEE IT WITH? _____

What did you like about this film?

_____


FILM NAME: _____

FAVORITE CHARACTER: _____

WHERE DID YOU SEE IT? _____

WHO DID YOU SEE IT WITH? _____

What did you like about this film?

_____


FILM NAME: _____

FAVORITE CHARACTER: _____

WHERE DID YOU SEE IT? _____

WHO DID YOU SEE IT WITH? _____

What did you like about this film?

_____

# YOUR LEAST FAVORITE

Book for young people:

_____

Color to wear:

_____

First lady:

_____

Grade in school:

_____

Kind of cake:

_____

Kind of pie:

_____

Perfume or cologne:

_____

President:

_____

Soup:

_____

Teacher:

_____

Thing to shop for:

_____

# YOUR MOST FAVORITE

Book for young people:

_____

Color to wear:

_____

First lady:

_____

Grade in school:

_____

Kind of cake:

_____

Kind of pie:

_____

Perfume or cologne:

_____

President:

_____

Soup:

_____

Teacher:

_____

Thing to shop for:

_____

# LAST NIGHT I . . . DREAMT:

### (LIST ALL OF THE PEOPLES, PLACES, AND THINGS YOU CAN
### REMEMBER FROM YOUR DREAMS LAST NIGHT)

DATE: _____

1. _____
2. _____
3. _____
4. _____
5. _____
6. _____
7. _____
8. _____
9. _____
10. _____
11. _____
12. _____
13. _____
14. _____
15. _____
16. _____

# YOUR LISTS

Things you'd do if you were invisible:

1. _____

2. _____

3. _____

4. _____

5. _____

Past civilizations you are interested in:

1. _____

2. _____

3. _____

4. _____

5. _____

Fictional or imaginary creatures you wish were real:

1. _____

2. _____

3. _____

4. _____

5. _____

# WHEN SOMEONE SAYS _____,
## YOU THINK . . .

Birdsong:

_____

Birth:

_____

Bitter:

_____

Blood:

_____

Bones:

_____

Boots:

_____

Bottles:

_____

Bracelet:

_____

Bread:

_____

Breath:

_____

Brick:

_____

# AT RANDOM

Are you good with remembering birthdays?
[ ] yes   [✓] no

Do you believe in magic?
[ ] yes   [ ] no

Do you consider yourself creative?
[✓] yes   [ ] no

Do you think you're attractive?
[✓] yes   [ ] no

Have you seen a ghost?
[ ] yes   [✓] no

Have you been more than 20 feet under water?
[ ] yes   [✓] no

Have you ridden on a train?
[✓] yes   [ ] no

Were any other names considered when it came to naming you?
[ ] yes   [ ] no

If that was a yes, what were they?

_____

_____

_____

_____

# MULTIPLE CHOICE

## WHICH OF THE FOLLOWING INTERESTS YOU MOST?

✓

____ Astronomy    ____ Biology
____ Geology    ____ Physics

____ Bass    ____ Drums
✓ Guitar    ____ Keyboards

✓ A fireplace    ____ A garden hot tub
____ A massage chair    ____ A surround-sound system

____ Baby showers    ____ Family reunions
____ Graduations    ____ Weddings

____ Architecture photography    ✓ Nature photography
____ Figurative photography    ____ Space photography

____ Betting games    ____ Card games
____ Dice games    ____ Domino games

____ Accounting    ____ Managing
____ Marketing    ____ Programming

____ Aliens    ✓ Conspiracy theories
____ Hauntings    ____ Mythology

---

You tend to sleep mostly on:
✓ Your back    ____ Your right side
____ Your left side    ____ Your stomach

In movies, you are most impressed by:
____ Lighting    ✓ Sets and design
____ Special effects    ____ Sound effects

## THIS OR THAT
### (CIRCLE YOUR PREFERENCE)

Socialism OR Capitalism

Buttons OR (Zippers)

Chess OR Checkers

(Diamonds) OR Pearls

Own land OR Own a house

(Ketchup) OR Mustard

Freud OR Jung

Bar soap OR (Shower gel)

Bubble wrap OR Packing peanuts

Debit OR Credit

Tap water OR (Bottled water)

(Whistling) OR Humming

Bright lights OR Soft lights

Have a job in a large company OR (Be your own boss)

One-story home OR Two-story home

Bare walls OR Busy walls

Slides OR (Swings)

Math OR (Spelling)

Regular-crust pizza OR (Thin-crust pizza)

Electric razor OR Disposable razor

Blinds OR Curtains

Shaken OR Stirred

Theme parks OR Fairs

Gelatin OR Pudding

(Patient) OR Impatient

(Bracelet) OR Necklaces

(Blanket) OR Comforter

# YOUR LISTS

Ice cream flavors you like:

1. _____
2. _____
3. _____
4. _____
5. _____
6. _____
7. _____
8. _____

Ice cream flavors you dislike:

1. _____
2. _____
3. _____
4. _____
5. _____
6. _____
7. _____
8. _____

The most overrated things in life:

1. _____
2. _____
3. _____
4. _____
5. _____
6. _____
7. _____
8. _____

The most underrated things in life:

1. _____
2. _____
3. _____
4. _____
5. _____
6. _____
7. _____
8. _____

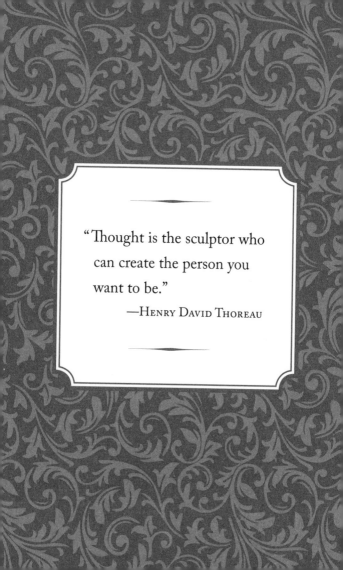

"Thought is the sculptor who can create the person you want to be."

—HENRY DAVID THOREAU

I am happy because . . .

## ON A SCALE OF 1 TO 10
### (CIRCLE YOUR PREFERENCE)

How important is physical beauty to you in a life partner?

1   2   3   4   5   6   (7)   8   9   10

How important is spontaneity to you in a life partner?

1   2   3   4   5   6   7   8   (9)   10

How important is tolerance to you in a life partner?

1   2   3   4   5   6   7   8   (9)   10

How important is sobriety to you in a life partner?

1   2   3   4   5   6   7   8   9   (10)

How important is playfulness to you in a life partner?

1   2   3   4   5   6   7   8   (9)   10

How important is ambition to you in a life partner?

1   2   3   4   5   6   7   (8)   9   10

How important is wealth to you in a life partner?

1   2   (3)   4   5   6   7   8   9   10

How important is cleanliness to you in a life partner?

1   2   3   4   5   6   7   (8)   9   10

# AT RANDOM

How do you prefer your coffee?

Cream and Sugar

What is your ring size?

Have you seen a shooting star?
[✔] yes  [ ] no

Are you good with remembering anniversaries?
[✔] yes  [ ] no

Do you usually remove the labels from your clothing?
[✔] yes  [ ] no

Did your parents care if you swore around them?
[ ] yes  [ ] no

Do you save the various greeting cards people give you?
[✔] yes  [ ] no

How many hours of sleep would you say you average per night?

Seven hours

Have you ever stayed up all night?
[✔] yes  [ ] no

# BOOK FAVORITES

BOOK TITLE: _____

AUTHOR: _____

FAVORITE CHARACTER: _____

FAVORITE SCENE: _____

What did you like about this book?

_____

_____


BOOK TITLE: _____

AUTHOR: _____

FAVORITE CHARACTER: _____

FAVORITE SCENE: _____

What did you like about this book?

_____

_____


BOOK TITLE: _____

AUTHOR: _____

FAVORITE CHARACTER: _____

FAVORITE SCENE: _____

What did you like about this book?

_____

_____

BOOK TITLE: _____

AUTHOR: _____

FAVORITE CHARACTER: _____

FAVORITE SCENE: _____

What did you like about this book?

_____

_____

BOOK TITLE: _____

AUTHOR: _____

FAVORITE CHARACTER: _____

FAVORITE SCENE: _____

What did you like about this book?

_____

_____

BOOK TITLE: _____

AUTHOR: _____

FAVORITE CHARACTER: _____

FAVORITE SCENE: _____

What did you like about this book?

_____

_____

# YOUR LISTS

Your pet peeves:

1. _____

2. _____

3. _____

4. _____

5. _____

6. _____

7. _____

8. _____


Your guilty pleasures:

1. _____

2. _____

3. _____

4. _____

5. _____

6. _____

7. _____

8. _____

Things you're obsessed with:

1. _____
2. _____
3. _____
4. _____
5. _____
6. _____
7. _____
8. _____

Things you worry about:

1. _____
2. _____
3. _____
4. _____
5. _____
6. _____
7. _____
8. _____

Words that best describe you:

1. _____

2. _____

3. _____

4. _____

5. _____

6. _____

New Year's resolutions you made and kept:

1. _____

2. _____

3. _____

4. _____

5. _____

6. _____

The best advice or tips you received, and from whom:

1. _____

2. _____

3. _____

4. _____

5. _____

6. _____

Medication or supplements you have taken this year:

1. _____
2. _____
3. _____
4. _____
5. _____
6. _____

Cereals you like:

1. _____
2. _____
3. _____
4. _____
5. _____
6. _____

Cereals you dislike:

1. _____
2. _____
3. _____
4. _____
5. _____
6. _____

# AT RANDOM

Has anyone written a song about you?
[  ] yes   [  ] no

Can you bake bread?
[✓] yes   [  ] no

Do you bruise easily?
[  ] yes   [✓] no

Have you visited a psychiatrist?
[  ] yes   [  ] no

Can you do a split?
[  ] yes   [✓] no

Do you like to swim?
[✓] yes   [  ] no

Have you been in a fist fight?
[✓] yes   [  ] no

Do you like seeing yourself in mirrors?
[✓] yes   [  ] no

Have you seriously considered joining the military?
[  ] yes   [✓] no

Would you mind if your best friend and your ex began dating?
[  ] yes   [  ] no

Have you ever talked on the phone for more than three
consecutive hours straight?
[✓] yes   [ ] no

If yes, with whom?

_____

Are you sometimes afraid to open your eyes in the dark?
[ ] yes   [✓] no

Do you believe prayer works?
[✓] yes   [ ] no

Have you changed a tire?
[ ] yes   [✓] no

Where do you like to sit when watching a movie in a theater?

_____

Who taught you how to drive?

_____

How many hours of sleep would you say you average
per night?
        Seven hours
_____

The favorite part of your body is:

_____

# YOUR LEAST FAVORITE

Chair type:

_____

Gum:

_____

Kind of coat:

_____

Reference book:

_____

Sports team:

_____

Stove:

_____

Swear word:

_____

Thing to talk about:

_____

Time of day to exercise:

_____

Word:

_____

Workout:

_____

# YOUR MOST FAVORITE

Chair type:

_____

Gum:

_____

Kind of coat:

_____

Reference book:

_____

Sports team:

_____

Stove:

_____

Swear word:

_____

Thing to talk about:

_____

Time of day to exercise:

_____

Word:

_____

Workout:

_____

# WHAT ARE YOUR THOUGHTS ON . . . ?

Acupuncture?

_____

_____

_____

_____

Global warming?

_____

_____

_____

_____

Infinity?

_____

_____

_____

_____

Public transportation?

_____

_____

_____

_____

# SUPERSTITIONS

Do you believe it's lucky to spill matches or light the last one in a matchbook?
[ ] yes  [ ] no

Do you believe it's bad luck to kill a spider?
[ ] yes  [ ] no

Do you believe it's unlucky to meet under mistletoe and not kiss the person?
[ ] yes  [ ] no

Do you believe it's unlucky to walk under a ladder?
[ ] yes  [ ] no

Do you believe that if you catch a falling leaf on the first day of autumn that you won't come down with a cold all winter?
[ ] yes  [ ] no

Do you believe that if someone gives you a pocket knife already open that you must give it back in the same manner?
[ ] yes  [ ] no

Do you believe that seeing a lone fox is lucky?
[ ] yes  [ ] no

Would you be afraid to camp out in a cemetery for a night?
[ ] yes  [ ] no

Do you believe that pulling out a gray hair will cause ten more to grow in its place?
[ ] yes  [ ] no

# WHEN SOMEONE SAYS _____,
## YOU THINK . . .

Bubbles:

_____

Butterflies:

_____

Cages:

_____

Calendars:

_____

Camouflage:

_____

Candles:

_____

Cards:

_____

Celebrity:

_____

Chaos:

_____

Cigarettes:

_____

Circles:

_____

# TODAY I . . . SPOKE TO:
(LIST ALL OF THE PEOPLE YOU
EXCHANGED WORDS WITH TODAY)

DATE: _____

1. _____

2. _____

3. _____

4. _____

5. _____

6. _____

7. _____

8. _____

9. _____

10. _____

11. _____

12. _____

13. _____

14. _____

15. _____

16. _____

# AT RANDOM

Types of wine you've tried (and circle your favorites):

| | |
|---|---|
| ___ Barbera | ___ Pinot Blanc |
| ___ Bordeaux | ___ Pinot Grigio |
| ___ Cabernet | ___ Pinot Noir |
| ___ Chablis | ___ Pinotage |
| ___ Champagne | ___ Port |
| ___ Chardonnay | ___ Prosecco |
| ___ Chenin Blanc | ___ Riesling |
| ___ Chianti | ___ Rosé |
| ___ Dolcetto | ___ Sangiovese |
| ___ Gewürztraminer | ___ Sauvignon Blanc |
| ___ Grenache | ___ Sémillon |
| ___ Kosher | ___ Sherry |
| ___ Madeira | ___ Syrah (shiraz) |
| ___ Marsanne | ___ Tempranillo |
| ___ Merlot | ___ Vermouth |
| ___ Muscat | ___ Viognier |
| ___ Nebbiolo | ___ Zinfandel |

The best meal you ever ate:

_____

Have you stayed awake for more than 48 hours straight?
[  ] yes   [✓] no

Have you worked more than 12 hours in a single day?
[  ] yes   [  ] no

Have you fallen asleep at work?
[  ] yes   [  ] no

The most money you've ever bet on something:

_____

If you could relive one moment of your life, which moment
would you choose?

_____

If you had an identical twin, would you ever trade places for fun?
[ ] yes  [ ] no

Are you still close to any of your grade school friends?
[ ] yes  [ ] no

Reasons you would watch the news:

____ A particular newscaster  ____ Positive messages

____ Celebrity gossip  ____ Stock market specifics

____ Consumer alerts  ____ Strange crimes

____ Crazy stories  ____ Traffic reports

____ Deaths  ____ Weather forecast

____ Political updates  ____ World events

Would you rather sleep alone or with someone else in the bed?

_____

If you could relive one moment of your life, which moment
would you choose?

_____

What mythical creature would you be, were it possible?

_____

# YOUR LEAST FAVORITE

Art form:

Bean:

Fish to eat:

Juice:

Number:

Sense:

Spice:

Song of summer:

Temperature:

Toothpaste:

World country:

# YOUR MOST FAVORITE

Art form:
_____

Bean:
_____

Fish to eat:
_____

Juice:
_____

Number:
_____

Sense:
_____

Spice:
_____

Song of summer:
_____

Temperature:
_____

Toothpaste:
_____

World country:
_____

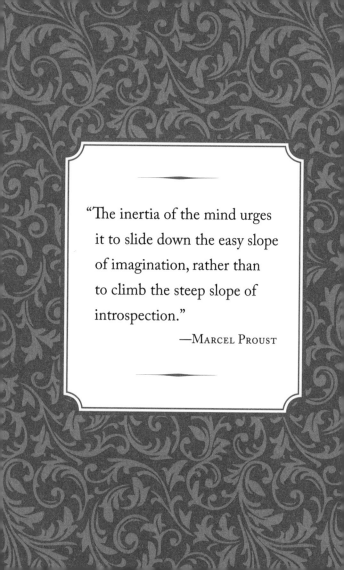

"The inertia of the mind urges
it to slide down the easy slope
of imagination, rather than
to climb the steep slope of
introspection."

—Marcel Proust

Right now I am thinking . . .

# THIS OR THAT
(CIRCLE YOUR PREFERENCE)

Waffles OR (Pancakes)

Head first OR (Feet first)

Truth OR (Dare)

(Salt) OR Pepper

Predictable OR (Spontaneous)

Forests OR (Fields)

(Snakes) OR Spiders

Fruits OR (Vegetables)

Rainbows OR Shooting stars

Lunar eclipse OR Solar eclipse

Bubbles OR Balloons

Business OR (Casual)

Stripes OR Polka dots

Massage OR Sleep

(Tan) OR Natural

Manicure OR Pedicure

(Quiet) OR Loud

Glasses OR Contacts

Sunblock OR Tanning oil

Scrambled OR (Fried)

(Young) OR Old

Stickers OR Stamps

Visual learning OR Auditory learning

(Test the water) OR Dive in

Tattoos OR Piercings

Safety OR (Danger)

Cursive OR (Print)

# YOUR LISTS

People who show up in your dreams:

1. _____

2. _____

3. _____

4. _____

5. _____

Facts that amaze you:

1. _____

2. _____

3. _____

4. _____

5. _____

Tattoos you would get:

1. _____

2. _____

3. _____

4. _____

5. _____

Classical composers you like:

1. _____
2. _____
3. _____
4. _____
5. _____
6. _____
7. _____
8. _____
9. _____

Classical composers you dislike:

1. _____
2. _____
3. _____
4. _____
5. _____
6. _____
7. _____
8. _____
9. _____

Nice things about being in a relationship:

1. _____

2. _____

3. _____

4. _____

5. _____

6. _____

7. _____

8. _____

9. _____


Challenging things about being in a relationship:

1. _____

2. _____

3. _____

4. _____

5. _____

6. _____

7. _____

8. _____

9. _____

# AT RANDOM

Do you like seeing live music?
[   ] yes   [   ] no

If yes, list the top five concerts you have seen, with your favorite first:

1. _____

2. _____

3. _____

4. _____

5. _____

6. _____

If no, list the top five concerts you would like to see, or wish you could have seen:

1. _____

2. _____

3. _____

4. _____

5. _____

6. _____

Something about human anatomy you'd change:

_____

You like for your home to smell like:

_____

How long can you run flat out without stopping?

_____

What color is the underwear you're currently wearing?

_____

Your height:

_____

The height you'd like to be:

_____

You'd like to live to be this age:

_____

If time travel were possible, would you visit the future or
the past and why?

_____

_____

_____

# VIDEO GAME FAVORITES

GAME TITLE: _____

CHARACTER: _____

PART: _____

FAVORITE SCENE: _____

Who or what does this game remind you of?

_____

_____


GAME TITLE: _____

CHARACTER: _____

PART: _____

FAVORITE SCENE: _____

Who or what does this game remind you of?

_____

_____


GAME TITLE: _____

CHARACTER: _____

PART: _____

FAVORITE SCENE: _____

Who or what does this game remind you of?

_____

_____

GAME TITLE: _____

CHARACTER: _____

PART: _____

FAVORITE SCENE: _____

Who or what does this game remind you of?

_____

_____


GAME TITLE: _____

CHARACTER: _____

PART: _____

FAVORITE SCENE: _____

Who or what does this game remind you of?

_____

_____


GAME TITLE: _____

CHARACTER: _____

PART: _____

FAVORITE SCENE: _____

Who or what does this game remind you of?

_____

_____

# YOUR LISTS

Future inventions you hope for:

1. _____
2. _____
3. _____
4. _____
5. _____

Gifts you would enjoy receiving:

1. _____
2. _____
3. _____
4. _____
5. _____

Things you wouldn't do for a billion dollars:

1. _____
2. _____
3. _____
4. _____
5. _____

# MULTIPLE CHOICE

You prefer to wear which of the following most often:

_____ Boxers          _____ Thongs

_____ Briefs          _____ Hipsters

_____ Bikini panties  _____ No underwear at all


You'd rather never have to do which one of the following again:

_____ Brush your teeth        _____ Laundry and dishes

_____ Wash and fix your hair  _____ Shave any part of your body


You believe which one of the following statements to be the truest:

_____ There are no coincidences

_____ Everything is a matter of chance

✓ It's all about balance

_____ There's no point in thinking about these sorts of things


If you had to live somewhere extreme, which of these would you choose:

_____ Living deep underground

_____ Living on another planet

_____ Living on a space station

_____ Living under an ocean


You're most like which one of the following types of people:

_____ I forgive and forget

_____ I hold a grudge

_____ I get even

✓ I don't take things too personally to begin with

# YOUR LEAST FAVORITE

Body part:

_____

Body shape:

_____

Car:

_____

Eye color:

_____

Fashion designer:

_____

Hair color:

_____

Place to walk:

_____

Politician:

_____

Restaurant:

_____

Store:

_____

Television commercial:

_____

# YOUR MOST FAVORITE

Body part:

_____

Body shape:

_____

Car:

_____

Eye color:

_____

Fashion designer:

_____

Hair color:

_____

Place to walk:

_____

Politician:

_____

Restaurant:

_____

Store:

_____

Television commercial:

_____

# SUPERSTITIONS

Would you feel uneasy opening an umbrella indoors?
[  ] yes   [  ] no

Do you avoid black cats?
[  ] yes   [  ] no

Do you believe finding a four-leaf clover is lucky?
[  ] yes   [  ] no

Would you feel uneasy putting your left shoe on before your right?
[  ] yes   [  ] no

Do you avoid walking on cracks in the sidewalk?
[  ] yes   [  ] no

Do you believe breaking a mirror will mean seven years bad luck?
[  ] yes   [  ] no

Do you believe carrying a rabbit's foot is lucky?
[  ] yes   [  ] no

Do you believe you can tell the sex of a child by whether or not the mother is carrying high or low?
[  ] yes   [  ] no

Do you believe eating black-eyed peas on
New Year's Day will bring you luck?
[  ] yes   [  ] no

Do you believe it is bad luck for the groom to see the bride before the wedding?
[  ] yes   [  ] no

# WHAT ARE YOUR THOUGHTS ON . . . ?

Physical education?

_____
_____
_____
_____

Art education?

_____
_____
_____
_____

College education?

_____
_____
_____
_____

Immigration?

_____
_____
_____
_____

# YOUR LISTS

Potions you'd make if magic were real:

1. _____

2. _____

3. _____

4. _____

5. _____

6. _____

7. _____

8. _____

Things you might go back and change or do if time travel was possible:

1. _____

2. _____

3. _____

4. _____

5. _____

6. _____

7. _____

8. _____

Blogs you like:

1. _____
2. _____
3. _____
4. _____
5. _____
6. _____
7. _____
8. _____

Blogs you dislike:

1. _____
2. _____
3. _____
4. _____
5. _____
6. _____
7. _____
8. _____

# AT RANDOM

Have you been overly infatuated with someone?
[✓] yes   [  ] no

Have you cried yourself to sleep?
[✓] yes   [  ] no

Have you felt an earthquake?
[  ] yes   [✓] no

Have you had a pen pal?
[✓] yes   [  ] no

Is your more photogenic side your right or your left?
_Left side_

Do you currently owe money to a friend or family member?
[✓] yes   [  ] no

How often do you shower or bathe?
_Once a week_

Have you ever tried maintaining a vegetarian diet?
[  ] yes   [✓] no

Do you believe in evolution?
[  ] yes   [✓] no

If you ever ended up on the news, you'd want it to be for:

The fastest you've ever driven:

_____

Do you believe Atlantis ever existed?

[ ] yes [ ] no

You believe love has more to do with which one of the
following:

____ Common interests    ____ Physical attraction
____ Dependency needs    ____ Timing and maturity level

Have you donated blood or plasma?
[ ] yes  [✓] no

Are you a donor?
[ ] yes  [✓] no

Do you believe in life after death?

[✓] yes [ ] no

What is the most important job you can think of anyone doing?

_____

How much do you think that job should pay annually?

_____

Have you been inside of a burning building?
[ ] yes  [✓] no

What happened?

_____

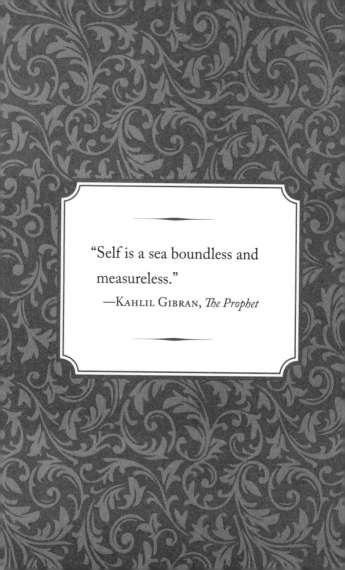

"Self is a sea boundless and measureless."

—Kahlil Gibran, *The Prophet*

I am inspired by . . .

# YOUR LISTS

Superpowers you'd enjoy having:

1. _____
2. _____
3. _____
4. _____
5. _____
6. _____
7. _____
8. _____

Things you'd have to have on a deserted island:

1. _____
2. _____
3. _____
4. _____
5. _____
6. _____
7. _____
8. _____

## WHEN SOMEONE SAYS _____,
## YOU THINK . . .

Clocks:

_____

Clouds:

_____

Clutter:

_____

Continent:

_____

Contradiction:

_____

Corporation:

_____

Cozy:

_____

Craft:

_____

Crooked:

_____

Crystal:

_____

Dancing:

_____

# ON A SCALE OF 1 TO 10

## (CIRCLE YOUR PREFERENCE)

How important is talent to you in a life partner?

1   2   3   4   5   6   7   8   9   10

How important is honesty to you in a life partner?

1   2   3   4   5   6   7   8   9   10

How important is generosity to you in a life partner?

1   2   3   4   5   6   7   8   9   10

How important is fitness to you in a life partner?

1   2   3   4   5   6   7   8   9   10

How important is discretion to you in a life partner?

1   2   3   4   5   6   7   8   9   10

How important is a sense of style to you in a life partner?

1   2   3   4   5   6   7   8   9   10

How important is affection to you in a life partner?

1   2   3   4   5   6   7   8   9   10

How important is decisiveness to you in a life partner?

1   2   3   4   5   6   7   8   9   10

# THIS OR THAT
### (CIRCLE YOUR PREFERENCE)

**Owls** OR Bats

**Delivery** OR Takeout

Solid deodorant OR **Gel deodorant**

**Boxing** OR Wrestling

Rice OR **Noodles**

**Ice cream** OR Sorbet

**Nuts** OR Raisins

**Red peppers** OR Green peppers

Being heard OR Being seen

Incandescent light OR Fluorescent light

Musicals OR **Dramas**

**Brush** OR Floss

Table OR **Booth**

**Smooth** OR Chunky

Makeup OR **Natural**

Be waited on OR Self-serve

Silk OR Suede

**Hardcover** OR Paperback

**Window seat** OR Aisle seat

Bottle OR Draft

**Take risks** OR Play it safe

Nail polish OR **No nail polish**

Manual transmission OR Automatic transmission

Real names OR Nicknames

Circuses OR **Rodeos**

Stand up OR Sit down

Cold cereal OR Hot cereal

# YOUR LEAST FAVORITE

Appliance:

_____

Article of clothing you own:

_____

Board game:

_____

Childhood memory:

_____

Childhood toy:

_____

College class:

_____

Commute:

_____

Doctor:

_____

Frozen yogurt flavor:

_____

Magazine:

_____

Social media site:

_____

# YOUR MOST FAVORITE

Appliance:

_____

Article of clothing you own:

_____

Board game:

_____

Childhood memory:

_____

Childhood toy:

_____

College class:

_____

Commute:

_____

Doctor:

_____

Frozen yogurt flavor:

_____

Magazine:

_____

Social media site:

_____

# AT RANDOM

Do you believe in reincarnation?
[  ] yes  [✓] no

Do you like roller coasters?
[✓] yes  [  ] no

Do you believe that your personality traits are determined
by your birthday?
[✓] yes  [  ] no

Have you dined alone at a restaurant?
[✓] yes  [  ] no

Have you eaten raw meat or fish?
[✓] yes  [  ] no

Have you kept a journal or diary?
[✓] yes  [  ] no

Have you been in a car accident?
[  ] yes  [✓] no

Have you lived alone?
[✓] yes  [  ] no

Have you been stung by a bee?
[✓] yes  [  ] no

Have you purchased something at a thrift store?
[✓] yes  [  ] no

Have you been to a professional sporting event?

[✓] yes   [ ] no

If you suddenly found yourself living in ancient times, you'd
survive by doing what?

_____

If you were a lawyer, what sort of people would you want to help?

_____

If you were to host or star in a TV show, which one would it be?

_____

If you could get away with any crime, what would it be?

_____

If you had to go streaking, you'd do it where?

_____

What do you wear to bed?

_____

The name of your favorite soap:

_____

The name of your favorite shampoo:

_____

# ASK SOMEONE

## THE NAME OF THE PERSON YOU'RE ASKING:

_____

In what part of the world do you imagine me being the happiest?

_____

What would you use to lure me into a trap?

_____

In a perfect world, who would I end up marrying?

_____

What is your favorite moment we've shared?

_____

What name do you think suits me better than my own?

_____

What things remind you of me?

_____

What do you hope I will always remember about you?

_____

# MULTIPLE CHOICE

You believe which one of the following statements to be the truest:

____ Nothing is promised, therefore it's every person for them self

____ The world owes you something

____ You owe the world something

_✓_ We're all connected and everything has relevance

Which of the following interests you most?

____ Baking    ____ Interior design

____ Gardening    _✓_ Journaling

You are most attracted to people born under the sign of:

____ Aries    ____ Libra

____ Taurus    ____ Scorpio

____ Gemini    ____ Sagittarius

____ Cancer    ____ Capricorn

____ Leo    ____ Aquarius

____ Virgo    ____ Pisces

Which of the following irritates you most?

____ Telemarketing    ____ Spam

____ Pop-ups    _✓_ Junk mail

Which of the following interests you most?

____ Lacrosse    ____ Track

____ Rugby    _✓_ Soccer

Where do you like to sit in the movie theater?

____ Up close    ____ Last row

_✓_ In the middle    ____ Balcony

# YOUR LISTS

Things you love that others seem to hate:

1. _____

2. _____

3. _____

4. _____

5. _____

Things that make you feel at ease:

1. _____

2. _____

3. _____

4. _____

5. _____

Quirky things about yourself:

1. _____

2. _____

3. _____

4. _____

5. _____

Elements of your dream wedding:

1. _____

2. _____

3. _____

4. _____

5. _____

6. _____

Things that remind you of home:

1. _____

2. _____

3. _____

4. _____

5. _____

6. _____

Things that make you uncomfortable:

1. _____

2. _____

3. _____

4. _____

5. _____

6. _____

U.S. states you have visited:

1. _____

2. _____

3. _____

4. _____

5. _____

6. _____

7. _____

8. _____

9. _____


U.S. states you'd like to visit:

1. _____

2. _____

3. _____

4. _____

5. _____

6. _____

7. _____

8. _____

9. _____

Condiments and dressings you like:

1. _____
2. _____
3. _____
4. _____
5. _____
6. _____
7. _____
8. _____
9. _____

Condiments and dressings you dislike:

1. _____
2. _____
3. _____
4. _____
5. _____
6. _____
7. _____
8. _____
9. _____

# AT RANDOM

Do you check your phone right after waking up?

[  ] yes  [  ] no

How many times a day do you check your cellphone?

_____

What was your very first email address?

_____

How often do you do laundry?

_____

How often do you do wash your hair?

_____

How often do you do take a nap?

_____

Have you ever won a game of pool?

[ ✓ ] yes  [  ] no

Have you seen a tornado with your own eyes?

[  ] yes  [ ✓ ] no

Have you been in a long-distance relationship?

[  ] yes  [  ] no

Have you seen a baby being born?

[ ] yes  [✓] no

Have you swum in the ocean?

[ ] yes  [ ] no

Have you snorkeled?

[ ] yes  [✓] no

Have you gone scubadiving?

[ ] yes  [✓] no

Have you gone sailing?

[ ] yes  [ ] no

Have you gone parasailing?

[ ] yes  [ ] no

Have you gone deep-sea fishing?

[ ] yes  [ ] no

Have you gone river or stream fishing?

[✓] yes  [ ] no

Have you gone ziplining?

[✓] yes  [ ] no

Have you gone rock climbing?

[ ] yes  [ ] no

Have you hitchhiked?

[ ] yes  [ ] no

# WHAT ARE YOUR THOUGHTS ON . . . ?

Religion?

_____

_____

_____

_____

Generic brands?

_____

_____

_____

_____

Wormholes?

_____

_____

_____

_____

Intimacy?

_____

_____

_____

_____

## WHEN SOMEONE SAYS _____,
## YOU THINK . . .

Danger:

_____

Desert:

_____

Deceit:

_____

Diamonds:

_____

Dirt:

_____

Disgust:

_____

Doozy:

_____

Dolls:

_____

Drama:

_____

Dream:

_____

Durable:

_____

"Healthy introspection, without undermining oneself; it is a rare gift to venture into the unexplored depths of the self . . . with an uncorrupted gaze."

—FRIEDRICH NIETZSCHE,
*Unpublished Writings from the Period of Unfashionable Observations*

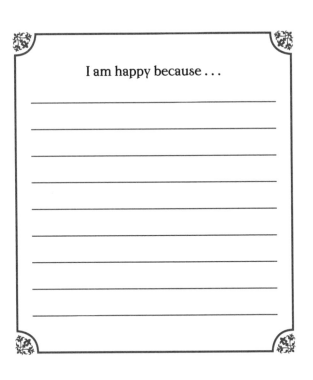

I am happy because . . .

# YOUR LISTS

Things you wish didn't exist:

1. _____

2. _____

3. _____

4. _____

5. _____


Reasons you visited or were in a hospital:

1. _____

2. _____

3. _____

4. _____

5. _____


Ways you break the ice with strangers:

1. _____

2. _____

3. _____

4. _____

5. _____

You think the world needs more:

1. _____
2. _____
3. _____
4. _____
5. _____
6. _____

Things you should never tell someone:

1. _____
2. _____
3. _____
4. _____
5. _____
6. _____

Pets you'd enjoy having:

1. _____
2. _____
3. _____
4. _____
5. _____
6. _____

# AT RANDOM

Have you had stitches?
[  ] yes   [√] no

Have you ever broken a bone?
[  ] yes   [√] no

                              Have you seen the Aurora Borealis?
                                       [  ] yes   [  ] no

Have you ridden in a taxi?
[√] yes   [  ] no

Have you ridden in a horse-drawn carriage?
[√] yes   [  ] no

Have you ever been on a blind date?
[  ] yes   [√] no

                              Have you taken part in a protest?
                                       [  ] yes   [  ] no

                              Have you ever signed a petition?
                                       [√] yes   [  ] no

Have you ever been fired?
[  ] yes   [  ] no

Why?

_____

Have you cut someone's hair?
[ ] yes  [ ] no

The shortest and longest lengths you've worn your hair are:

_____

Have you ever placed an ad?
[ ] yes  [ ] no

Have you ever answered an ad?
[ ] yes  [ ] no

Have you ever had too much to drink?
[ ] yes  [ ] no

Have you ever made a prank call?
[ ] yes  [ ] no

Have you been hunting?
[√] yes  [ ] no

Have you ever been stranded in a car that broke down?
[ ] yes  [ ] no

Have you used jumper cables to start a car?
[√] yes  [ ] no

Have you performed on stage?
[ ] yes  [ ] no

Describe the performance:

_____

_____

## THIS OR THAT
### (CIRCLE YOUR PREFERENCE)

Visit Mars OR Visit the moon

Sketching OR Detailed drawing

Freshwater fish OR Saltwater fish

Daytime talks shows OR Late-night talk shows

Play for fun OR Play to win

Electric guitar OR Acoustic guitar

Hard candy OR Chewy candy

Solo sport OR Team sport

Jeans OR Sweats

Watches OR Clocks

Elevator OR Stairs

Batting cage OR Mini golf

Firm pillow OR Down pillow

Firm mattress OR Soft mattress

Gas grill OR Charcoal grill

Large parties OR Small gatherings

Cold drinks OR Hot drinks

Pawn OR Sell

Flower bouquets OR Potted plants

Comic strips OR Graphic novels

Darts OR Ping pong

Cloudy OR Windy

Heavy snow OR Light snow

Baked potatoes OR Mashed potatoes

Crushed ice OR Ice cubes

Sugar OR Sugar-free sweetener

Ceiling fan OR Window fan

# TODGY I . . . ATE AND DRANK:

(LIST ALL OF THE FOOD AND DRINKS YOU HAD
THIS DAY, AND WHERE)

DATE: _____

1. _____ at _____

2. _____ at _____

3. _____ at _____

4. _____ at _____

5. _____ at _____

6. _____ at _____

7. _____ at _____

8. _____ at _____

9. _____ at _____

10. _____ at _____

11. _____ at _____

12. _____ at _____

13. _____ at _____

14. _____ at _____

15. _____ at _____

# YOUR LISTS

Things you would buy with a million dollars:

1. _____
2. _____
3. _____
4. _____
5. _____
6. _____
7. _____
8. _____

Charities you would donate to:

1. _____
2. _____
3. _____
4. _____
5. _____
6. _____
7. _____
8. _____

Conferences you have been to:

1. _____

2. _____

3. _____

4. _____

5. _____

6. _____

7. _____

8. _____


Reasons you've been late for school or work:

1. _____

2. _____

3. _____

4. _____

5. _____

6. _____

7. _____

8. _____

Beers you like:

1. _____
2. _____
3. _____
4. _____
5. _____
6. _____
7. _____
8. _____
9. _____

Beers you dislike:

1. _____
2. _____
3. _____
4. _____
5. _____
6. _____
7. _____
8. _____
9. _____

# ON A SCALE OF 1 TO 10
## (CIRCLE YOUR PREFERENCE)

How important is a sense of adventure to you in a life partner?

1   2   3   4   5   6   7   8   9   10

How important is flexibility to you in a life partner?

1   2   3   4   5   6   7   8   9   10

How important is availability to you in a life partner?

1   2   3   4   5   6   7   8   9   10

How important is humility to you in a life partner?

1   2   3   4   5   6   7   8   9   10

How important is libido to you in a life partner?

1   2   3   4   5   6   7   8   9   10

How important is religiosity to you in a life partner?

1   2   3   4   5   6   7   8   9   10

How important is tact to you in a life partner?

1   2   3   4   5   6   7   8   9   10

How important is curiosity to you in a life partner?

1   2   3   4   5   6   7   8   9   10

# MORE MUSIC FAVORITES:
## SOLO MALE SINGERS

ARTIST NAME: _____

ALBUM: _____

SONG: _____

Who or what memory does this song remind you of?

_____

_____


ARTIST NAME: _____

ALBUM: _____

SONG: _____

Who or what memory does this song remind you of?

_____

_____


ARTIST NAME: _____

ALBUM: _____

SONG: _____

Who or what memory does this song remind you of?

_____

_____

# MORE MUSIC FAVORITES:
## SOLO FEMALE SINGERS

ARTIST NAME: _____

ALBUM: _____

SONG: _____

Who or what memory does this song remind you of?

_____

_____


ARTIST NAME: _____

ALBUM: _____

SONG: _____

Who or what memory does this song remind you of?

_____

_____


ARTIST NAME: _____

ALBUM: _____

SONG: _____

Who or what memory does this song remind you of?

_____

_____

# AT RANDOM

Have you ever danced like no one was watching?
[  ] yes   [  ] no

The most fun you ever had dancing with someone was with this
person, this kind of dance, at this place:

_____

_____

Have you ever used a tanning bed?
[  ] yes   [  ] no

Do you chew gum?
[✓] yes   [  ] no

Have you ever smoked a cigar?
[  ] yes   [✓] no

Have you ever smoked an e-cigarette?
[  ] yes   [✓] no

Have you ever smoked a regular cigarette?
[  ] yes   [✓] no

If yes do you still smoke?
[  ] yes   [  ] no

If yes have you ever tried quitting?
[  ] yes   [  ] no

How many times have you tried?

_____

Have you purchased something online?
[√] yes   [ ] no

Have you ever been part of a love triangle?
[ ] yes   [ ] no

Did you have a stuffed animal you loved as a child?
[√] yes   [ ] no

What kind, and what was its name?

_____

How many addresses have you lived at?

_____

Name the streets and towns of those addresses, and the
approximate years you lived there:

_____

_____

_____

_____

_____

_____

# YOUR LEAST FAVORITE

Game show:

_____

Meat:

_____

Professional athlete:

_____

Aspect of your house:

_____

Flower:

_____

Tree:

_____

Bird:

_____

Cartoon:

_____

Fruit:

_____

Fast-food item:

_____

Film sequel:

_____

# YOUR MOST FAVORITE

Game show:

_____

Meat:

_____

Professional athlete:

_____

Aspect of your house:

_____

Flower:

_____

Tree:

_____

Bird:

_____

Cartoon:

_____

Fruit:

_____

Fast-food item:

_____

Film sequel:

_____

# SUPERSTITIONS

Do you believe that someone who cuts bread in an uneven manner has recently been lying?
[ ] yes  [ ] no

Do you believe that hanging wind chimes in or around your home will keep evil spirits at bay?
[ ] yes  [ ] no

Would you feel uneasy if you saw an owl during the daylight?
[ ] yes  [ ] no

Would you feel uneasy if a candle went out without human interaction?
[ ] yes  [ ] no

Do you ever cross your fingers when you wish, hope or lie?
[ ] yes  [ ] no

Do you believe kissing someone at midnight on New Year's Eve will bring you closer to them?
[ ] yes  [ ] no

Do you ever pick a seeded dandelion and try to blow all the seeds off in an effort to make a wish come true?
[ ] yes  [ ] no

Do you ever place a fallen eyelash between your thumb and forefinger, guess at which finger it will be on when you pull your fingers apart, and then make a wish if you guessed correctly?
[ ] yes  [ ] no

# WHAT ARE YOUR THOUGHTS ON . . . ?

Cosmetic surgery?

_____

_____

_____

_____

Voting?

_____

_____

_____

_____

Streaming music?

_____

_____

_____

_____

Online dating?

_____

_____

_____

_____

# AT RANDOM

What do you like to do on your birthday?

_____

_____

Do you have a famous relative?
[  ] yes   [  ] no

If yes, who are they?

_____

_____

                    Do plain white walls freak you out?
                              [  ] yes   [  ] no

Did you ever pretend to be sick so you didn't have
to go to school?
[  ] yes   [  ] no

Do you cuss freely outside of mixed company?
[  ] yes   [  ] no

If you had to say hell was somewhere on Earth, where
would you claim it to be?

_____

The name of the best cook you know:

_____

Have you completed your income taxes by yourself?
[  ] yes   [  ] no

Do you believe aliens had anything to do with
the creationof Stonehenge?
[  ] yes   [  ] no

Do you believe Bigfoot exists?
[  ] yes   [  ] no

Do you believe the Loch Ness Monster exists?
[  ] yes   [  ] no

Have you played the lottery?
[  ] yes   [  ] no

If yes, have you won? How much?

_____

Do your friends tend to be mostly males or females?

_____

If you could change one thing about human nature,
what would it be?

_____

"When Thales was asked what was difficult, he said, 'To know one's self.'"

—Diogenes Laërtius

Right now I am thinking . . .

_____

_____

_____

_____

_____

_____

_____

_____

_____

# YOUR LISTS

Questions you'd like answers to:

1. _____
2. _____
3. _____
4. _____
5. _____
6. _____
7. _____
8. _____

Rules you live your life by:

1. _____
2. _____
3. _____
4. _____
5. _____
6. _____
7. _____
8. _____

Things you're allergic to or had an allergic reaction to:

1. _____
2. _____
3. _____
4. _____
5. _____
6. _____

Things you miss about being a child:

1. _____
2. _____
3. _____
4. _____
5. _____
6. _____

Things you learned that you never used:

1. _____
2. _____
3. _____
4. _____
5. _____
6. _____

## WHEN SOMEONE SAYS _____,
## YOU THINK . . .

Earthy:
_____

Easy:
_____

Ecstatic:
_____

Educated:
_____

Effort:
_____

Eggs:
_____

Elevator:
_____

Energetic:
_____

Examination:
_____

Exhaustion:
_____

Exotic:
_____

# AT RANDOM

How many pairs of shoes do you own?

_____

Do you think there was or is life on Mars?

_____

Do you pluck your eyebrows?
[ √ ] yes  [  ] no

Have you been bitten by a spider or snake?
[  ] yes  [  ] no

How do you get rid of hiccups?

_____

Have you had surgery?
[  ] yes  [ √ ] no

Have you made fire without the help of a lighter, a match,
or any form of electricity?
[  ] yes  [  ] no

Have you gone more than a week without using a phone?
[ √ ] yes  [  ] no

A day?
[ √ ] yes  [  ] no

# MULTIPLE CHOICE

What would be your ideal floor of a multistory apartment building to live on?

\_\_\_\_Ground floor    \_\_\_\_Somewhere in the middle

\_\_\_\_Second floor    \_\_\_\_Highest floor or penthouse

You prefer to sleep:

\_\_\_\_Naked    _✓_ In pajamas

\_\_\_\_In underwear    \_\_\_\_In a T-shirt

You like your eggs:

\_\_\_\_Over easy    \_\_\_\_Boiled (hard or soft)

\_\_\_\_Scrambled    \_\_\_\_Poached

You are most interested in:

\_\_\_\_Buddy films    \_\_\_\_Musical films

\_\_\_\_Chick flicks    \_\_\_\_Foreign films

Your ideal vacation would be:

\_\_\_\_A ski resort    \_\_\_\_A countryside or camping trip

\_\_\_\_A beach resort    \_\_\_\_A city trip

\_\_\_\_A volunteer program    \_\_\_\_A wine-tasting trip

You think the smartest animal on earth is:

\_\_\_\_Dolphin    \_\_\_\_Whale    _✓_ Dog    \_\_\_\_Monkey or ape

Your fantasy career would be:

\_\_\_\_Rock star    \_\_\_\_Famous architect

\_\_\_\_Revered politician    \_\_\_\_Famous artist

\_\_\_\_Famous athlete    \_\_\_\_Famous writer or journalist

\_\_\_\_Famous scientist    \_\_\_\_Famous fashion designer

_✓_ Famous entrepreneur    \_\_\_\_Famous chef

# TODO I . . . WENT TO:

### (LIST ALL OF THE PLACES YOU WENT TODAY)

DATE: _____

1. _____
2. _____
3. _____
4. _____
5. _____
6. _____
7. _____
8. _____
9. _____
10. _____
11. _____
12. _____
13. _____
14. _____
15. _____
16. _____

# YOUR LISTS

Words you like:

1. _____
2. _____
3. _____
4. _____
5. _____
8. _____
7. _____
8. _____

Words you absolutely hate:

1. _____
2. _____
3. _____
4. _____
5. _____
8. _____
7. _____
8. _____

The most attractive people you've known:

1. _____
2. _____
3. _____
4. _____
5. _____
6. _____

Dishes common to your family meals:

1. _____
2. _____
3. _____
4. _____
5. _____
6. _____

The first books you remember reading:

1. _____
2. _____
3. _____
4. _____
5. _____
6. _____

Foods you've always wanted to try:

1. _____
2. _____
3. _____
4. _____
5. _____
8. _____
7. _____
8. _____
9. _____

Foods you refuse to try:

1. _____
2. _____
3. _____
4. _____
5. _____
8. _____
7. _____
8. _____
9. _____

# TELEVISION FAVORITES:
## CHILD ACTORS AND ACTRESSES

SHOW TITLE: _____

ACTOR NAME: _____

What is endearing or impressive about this child actor or actress?

_____

_____


SHOW TITLE: _____

ACTOR NAME: _____

What is endearing or impressive about this child actor or actress?

_____

_____


SHOW TITLE: _____

ACTOR NAME: _____

What is endearing or impressive about this child actor or actress?

_____

_____


SHOW TITLE: _____

ACTOR NAME: _____

What is endearing or impressive about this child actor or actress?

_____

_____

# TELEVISION FAVORITES: ACTORS

SHOW TITLE: _____

ACTOR NAME: _____

What do you like about this actor?

_____

_____


SHOW TITLE: _____

ACTOR NAME: _____

What do you like about this actor?

_____

_____


SHOW TITLE: _____

ACTOR NAME: _____

What do you like about this actor?

_____

_____


SHOW TITLE: _____

ACTOR NAME: _____

What do you like about this actor?

_____

_____

# TELEVISION FAVORITES: ACTRESSES

SHOW TITLE: _____

ACTRESS NAME: _____

What do you like about this actress?

_____

_____


SHOW TITLE: _____

ACTRESS NAME: _____

What do you like about this actress?

_____

_____


SHOW TITLE: _____

ACTRESS NAME: _____

What do you like about this actress?

_____

_____


SHOW TITLE: _____

ACTRESS NAME: _____

What do you like about this actress?

_____

_____

# AT RANDOM

Have you had a close friend confess their love for you?
[ ] yes   [ ] no

Is a prenuptial agreement important to you when considering marriage?
[ ] yes   [ ] no

Did you attend your high school prom?
[ ] yes   [ ] no

Have you lied about your age?
[ ] yes   [ ] no

How do you behave or feel when you're nervous?

_____

_____

How do you behave or feel when you're excited?

_____

_____

Are you ticklish?
[ ] yes   [ ] no

If yes, where is your most ticklish spot?

_____

## ON A SCALE OF 1 TO 10
### (CIRCLE YOUR PREFERENCE)

How important is independence to you in a life partner?

1    2    3    4    5    6    7    8    9    10

How important is posture to you in a life partner?

1    2    3    4    5    6    7    8    9    10

How important is cautiousness to you in a life partner?

1    2    3    4    5    6    7    8    9    10

How important is sensitivity to you in a life partner?

1    2    3    4    5    6    7    8    9    10

How important is uniqueness to you in a life partner?

1    2    3    4    5    6    7    8    9    10

How important is courtesy to you in a life partner?

1    2    3    4    5    6    7    8    9    10

How important is a sense of romance to you in a life partner?

1    2    3    4    5    6    7    8    9    10

How important is intellectualism to you in a life partner?

1    2    3    4    5    6    7    8    9    10

# AT RANDOM

How many books do you estimate you have read thus far?

_____

Do you usually make it a point to carry cash on you?
[  ] yes   [  ] no

Have you used a level to hang something?
[  ] yes   [  ] no

Were you ever held back a year in grade school?
[  ] yes   [  ] no

Were you ever moved ahead a year in grade school?
[  ] yes   [  ] no

Do you tend to take your work home with you?
[  ] yes   [  ] no

If you had to have plastic surgery, what would you have done?

_____

Do you know how to properly eat food with chopsticks?
[  ] yes   [  ] no

Have you rented a vehicle?
[  ] yes   [  ] no

Have you been skinny-dipping?
[  ] yes   [  ] no

Have you been on a ship?

[ ] yes   [ ] no

Have you ever had a near-death experience?

[ ] yes   [ ] no

If yes, what happened?

_____

_____

_____

Have you won a contest?

[ ] yes   [ ] no

Have you owned a public library card?

[ ] yes   [ ] no

Have you gone more than a week without watching TV?

[ ] yes   [ ] no

Have you fainted?

[ ] yes   [ ] no

Have you been on an airplane?

[ ] yes   [ ] no

Your longest flight was:

_____

Have you had a hickey?

[ ] yes   [ ] no

# MORE MUSIC FAVORITES: GROUPS

GROUP NAME: _____

ALBUM: _____

SONG: _____

Who or what memory does this song remind you of?

_____

_____


GROUP NAME: _____

ALBUM: _____

SONG: _____

Who or what memory does this song remind you of?

_____

_____


GROUP NAME: _____

ALBUM: _____

SONG: _____

Who or what memory does this song remind you of?

_____

_____

## THIS OR THAT
(CIRCLE YOUR PREFERENCE)

Love OR Money

Top bunk OR Bottom bunk

Chocolate OR Vanilla

High-maintenance OR Low-maintenance

Coffee OR Tea

Stoplights OR Heavy traffic

Hugs OR Kisses

Sunrise OR Sunset

Taking pictures OR Being in pictures

Conservative OR Liberal

Introvert OR Extrovert

Paper OR Plastic

Caffeine OR Sugar

Lake OR Ocean

Morning shower OR Evening shower

Right-handed OR Left-handed

Gold OR Silver

Day OR Night

Car OR Truck

Moon OR Stars

Travel OR Rest

Romance OR Directness

Friday nights OR Sunday mornings

Hot dog OR Hamburger

A cleaning robot OR A cooking robot

Roller skates OR Rollerblades

Diet OR Exercise

"You shall not look through my eyes
    either, nor take things from me,
You shall listen to all sides and
    filter them from your self.

. . . . . . . . . . . . . . . . . . . . . . . . . . . . . .

One world is aware and by far the
    largest to me, and that is myself,
And whether I come to my own
    to-day or in ten thousand or ten
    million years,
I can cheerfully take it now, or with
    equal cheerfulness I can wait."
        —WALT WHITMAN, *Song of Myself*

I am inspired by . . .

# WHAT ARE YOUR THOUGHTS ON . . . ?

Pennies?

_____

_____

_____

_____

Hollywood?

_____

_____

_____

_____

Reality television?

_____

_____

_____

_____

Singing or dancing television contests?

_____

_____

_____

_____

# WHEN SOMEONE SAYS _____,
## YOU THINK . . .

False:
_____

Fans:
_____

Farthest:
_____

Feathers:
_____

Fever:
_____

Fireplaces:
_____

Flags:
_____

Flannel:
_____

Fog:
_____

Fossils:
_____

Funny:
_____

# YOUR LISTS

Memorable things about your birth decade:

1. _____

2. _____

3. _____

4. _____

5. _____

6. _____

7. _____

8. _____

Your favorite family traditions:

1. _____

2. _____

3. _____

4. _____

5. _____

6. _____

7. _____

8. _____

Things you weren't taught in grade school:

1. _____

2. _____

3. _____

4. _____

5. _____

6. _____

Great songs for a graduation ceremony:

1. _____

2. _____

3. _____

4. _____

5. _____

6. _____

Things you forgot after you graduated:

1. _____

2. _____

3. _____

4. _____

5. _____

6. _____

Names you'd give or have given to pets:

1. _____
2. _____
3. _____
4. _____
5. _____
6. _____

Foreign countries you've visited:

1. _____
2. _____
3. _____
4. _____
5. _____
6. _____

Theme parties you would like to go to:

1. _____
2. _____
3. _____
4. _____
5. _____
6. _____

Things that make a person successful:

1. _____
2. _____
3. _____
4. _____
5. _____
6. _____
7. _____
8. _____
9. _____
10. _____

The best parts of your average day:

1. _____
2. _____
3. _____
4. _____
5. _____
6. _____
7. _____
8. _____
9. _____
10. _____

# LAST NIGHT I . . . DREAMT:

### (LIST ALL OF THE PEOPLES, PLACES, AND THINGS YOU CAN REMEMBER FROM YOUR DREAMS LAST NIGHT)

DATE: _____

1. _____

2. _____

3. _____

4. _____

5. _____

6. _____

7. _____

8. _____

9. _____

10. _____

11. _____

12. _____

13. _____

14. _____

15. _____

16. _____

# AT RANDOM

How often do you brush your teeth?

_____

The name of your favorite toothpaste:

_____

Have you used a toothbrush that wasn't your own?
[ ] yes   [ ] no

Have you gone a week or more without bathing or showering?

_____

How many times per day do you usually eat?

_____

What is your favorite meal of the day?

_____

Your favorite guilty treat?

_____

Your least-favorite foods as a child?

_____

_____

# MORE FILM FAVORITES: CLASSIC MOVIES

FILM NAME: _____

FAVORITE CHARACTER: _____

WHERE DID YOU SEE IT? _____

WHO DID YOU SEE IT WITH? _____

What did you like about this film?

_____

_____


FILM NAME: _____

FAVORITE CHARACTER: _____

WHERE DID YOU SEE IT? _____

WHO DID YOU SEE IT WITH? _____

What did you like about this film?

_____

_____


FILM NAME: _____

FAVORITE CHARACTER: _____

WHERE DID YOU SEE IT? _____

WHO DID YOU SEE IT WITH? _____

What did you like about this film?

_____

_____

FILM NAME: _____

FAVORITE CHARACTER: _____

WHERE DID YOU SEE IT? _____

WHO DID YOU SEE IT WITH? _____

What did you like about this film?

_____

_____


FILM NAME: _____

FAVORITE CHARACTER: _____

WHERE DID YOU SEE IT? _____

WHO DID YOU SEE IT WITH? _____

What did you like about this film?

_____

_____


FILM NAME: _____

FAVORITE CHARACTER: _____

WHERE DID YOU SEE IT? _____

WHO DID YOU SEE IT WITH? _____

What did you like about this film?

_____

_____

# ON A SCALE OF 1 TO 10
### (CIRCLE YOUR PREFERENCE)

How important is punctuality to you in a friend?

1    2    3    4    5    6    7    8    9    10

How important is a sense of humor to you in a friend?

1    2    3    4    5    6    7    8    9    10

How important is creativity to you in a friend?

1    2    3    4    5    6    7    8    9    10

How important is loyalty to you in a friend?

1    2    3    4    5    6    7    8    9    10

How important is kindness to you in a friend?

1    2    3    4    5    6    7    8    9    10

How important is frugality to you in a friend?

1    2    3    4    5    6    7    8    9    10

How important is spontaneity to you in a friend?

1    2    3    4    5    6    7    8    9    10

How important is tolerance to you in a friend?

1    2    3    4    5    6    7    8    9    10

# SUPERSTITIONS

Do you knock on wood for luck?
[  ] yes   [  ] no

Do you believe that dreaming of fish means someone you
know is pregnant?
[  ] yes   [  ] no

Do you believe it unlucky to take a shot of liquor without first
tapping the shot glass on a countertop?
[  ] yes   [  ] no

Do you believe that whoever catches the bride's bouquet
will be the next to marry?
[  ] yes   [  ] no

Would you feel compelled to throw money into a fountain or
well and make a wish if you came across one?
[  ] yes   [  ] no

Would you feel uneasy falling asleep with your feet uncovered?
[  ] yes   [  ] no

Do you believe the four of clubs is an unlucky card to
have in your hand?
[  ] yes   [  ] no

Do you believe you can know how many children you will
have by cutting an apple in half and counting the seeds?
[  ] yes   [  ] no

Do you make a wish when you see a shooting star?
[  ] yes   [  ] no

## THIS OR THAT
(CIRCLE YOUR PREFERENCE)

Alarm clock OR Wake naturally

Psychic abilities OR Telekinetic abilities

Multiply OR Divide

Olives OR Onions

Headphones OR Ear buds

White gravy OR Brown gravy

Sky diving OR Bungee jumping

Competing OR Spectating

Garlic OR Ginger

Holidays OR Regular days

Potato chip OR Corn chip

e-calendar OR Paper datebook

Adventure OR Comfort

Fiction OR Nonfiction

e-greeting cards OR Paper cards

Picnics OR Restaurant lunches

Under OR Over

Ancient Egypt OR Ancient Rome

Socks with shoes OR No socks with shoes

Bronze statues OR Marble statues

Tinted sunglasses OR Mirrored sunglasses

Rembrandt OR Michelangelo

Herbal tea OR Caffeinated tea

Convertible OR Closed top

Cricket sounds OR Frog sounds

Work too much OR Not work enough

Wooden fence OR Chain-link fence

# AT RANDOM

Has anyone given you flowers?
[   ] yes   [   ] no

Have you ever given someone flowers?
[   ] yes   [   ] no

What is your favorite kind of apple?

_____

What is your favorite place to be alone:

_____

How long can you hold your breath underwater?

_____

Have you made your own beer or wine?
[   ] yes   [   ] no

Your lucky number is:

_____

Why?

_____

_____

# MULTIPLE CHOICE

## WHICH OF THE FOLLOWING INTERESTS YOU MOST?

You'd rather attend which one of the following:

____ A ballet      ____ A dramatic play      ____ A circus

____ A musical      ____ A symphony      ____ An opera

____ A poetry reading      ____ A rock concert      ____ A lecture

____ A puppet show

You are most scared of which weather phenomenon:

____ Blizzards      ____ Hurricanes      ____ Earthquakes

____ Tornados      ____ Floods      ____ Volcanic eruptions

Your favorite room in your home is:

____ Kitchen      ____ Living room      ____ Bathroom

____ Study      ____ Bedroom      ____ Family room

____ Dining room      ____ Garage

If I could play a musical instrument it would

____ Piano      ____ Cello      ____ Violin      ____ Saxophone

____ Guitar      ____ Drums      ____ Flute      ____ Trumpet

Your favorite type of interior design is:

____ Country-style      ____ Mid-century modern

____ Contemporary      ____ Ethnic

____ Super modern      ____ Eclectic mix of old and new

You would describe your fashion sense as:

____ Classic      ____ Athletic      ____ Preppy

____ Bohemian      ____ Punk      ____ Modern, edgy

____ Goth      ____ Futuristic

# WHAT ARE YOUR THOUGHTS ON . . . ?

Cleanses?

_____

_____

_____

_____

Paparazzi?

_____

_____

_____

_____

Classified information?

_____

_____

_____

_____

Popularity?

_____

_____

_____

_____

Self-reverence, self-knowledge, self-control,—

These three alone lead life to sovereign power.

—Lord Alfred Tennyson, *"Œnone"*

I am happy because . . .

_____

_____

_____

_____

_____

_____

_____

_____

# YOUR LISTS

Books or comics you'd like seen made into movies:

1. _____
2. _____
3. _____
4. _____
5. _____
6. _____
7. _____
8. _____


Chores you hate doing, in order of least favorite first:

1. _____
2. _____
3. _____
4. _____
5. _____
6. _____
7. _____
8. _____

Topics you typically avoid in conversation:

1. _____

2. _____

3. _____

4. _____

5. _____

6. _____

People always tell you that you resemble which celebrity:

1. _____

2. _____

3. _____

4. _____

5. _____

6. _____

Things that offend you:

1. _____

2. _____

3. _____

4. _____

5. _____

6. _____

# TODAY I . . . WATCHED:

(LIST ALL OF THE VIDEOS, SHOWS, OR MOVIES YOU
WATCHED ONLINE, STREAMING, ON TV, OR AT A CINEMA)

**DATE:** _____

1. _____
2. _____
3. _____
4. _____
5. _____
6. _____
7. _____
8. _____
9. _____
10. _____
11. _____
12. _____
13. _____
14. _____
15. _____
16. _____

# WHEN SOMEONE SAYS _____,
## YOU THINK . . .

Garlic:
_____

Gate:
_____

Gaze:
_____

Gelatin:
_____

Gesture:
_____

Gimmick:
_____

Giving:
_____

God:
_____

Gossip:
_____

Gravity:
_____

Guilt:
_____

# MORE BOOK FAVORITES: CLASSIC NOVELS

BOOK TITLE: _____

AUTHOR: _____

FAVORITE CHARACTER: _____

FAVORITE SCENE: _____

What did you like about this book?

_____

_____


BOOK TITLE: _____

AUTHOR: _____

FAVORITE CHARACTER: _____

FAVORITE SCENE: _____

What did you like about this book?

_____

_____


BOOK TITLE: _____

AUTHOR: _____

FAVORITE CHARACTER: _____

FAVORITE SCENE: _____

What did you like about this book?

_____

_____

BOOK TITLE: _____

AUTHOR: _____

FAVORITE CHARACTER: _____

FAVORITE SCENE: _____

What did you like about this book?

_____

_____

BOOK TITLE: _____

AUTHOR: _____

FAVORITE CHARACTER: _____

FAVORITE SCENE: _____

What did you like about this book?

_____

_____

BOOK TITLE: _____

AUTHOR: _____

FAVORITE CHARACTER: _____

FAVORITE SCENE: _____

What did you like about this book?

_____

_____

# YOUR LISTS

Free things you enjoy doing:

1. _____
2. _____
3. _____
4. _____
5. _____
6. _____
7. _____
8. _____

Gifts you'd give, and to whom, if you won the lottery:

1. _____
2. _____
3. _____
4. _____
5. _____
6. _____
7. _____
8. _____

Best dressers you know:

1. _____
2. _____
3. _____
4. _____
5. _____
6. _____
7. _____
8. _____

Scents you like (candles, perfume, food aromas):

1. _____
2. _____
3. _____
4. _____
5. _____
6. _____
7. _____
8. _____

## THIS OR THAT
### (CIRCLE YOUR PREFERENCE)

Match OR Lighter

Song verses OR Song choruses

Fake plants OR Real plants

Shampoo OR Conditioner

Taco OR Burrito

Guacamole OR Salsa

Biscuits OR Cornbread

A tactical approach OR A forceful approach

Bingo OR Slot machine

Trick OR Treat

Lipstick OR Lip balm

Mass transportation OR Car or taxi

Map OR Compass

Mexican food OR Indian food

Foosball OR Air hockey

Tomato sauce OR Alfredo sauce

Bugs that fly OR Bugs that crawl

Unicorns OR Dragons

Glossy OR Matte

Chicken OR Tofu

North OR South

Tablet OR Capsule

Rocks OR Neat

Ballpoint OR Gel

Speedwalk OR Stroll

June OR September

December OR January

# ON A SCALE OF 1 TO 10
## (CIRCLE YOUR PREFERENCE)

How important is playfulness to you in a friend?

1   2   3   4   5   6   7   8   9   10

How important is wealth to you in a friend?

1   2   3   4   5   6   7   8   9   10

How important is ambition to you in a friend?

1   2   3   4   5   6   7   8   9   10

How important is generosity to you in a friend?

1   2   3   4   5   6   7   8   9   10

How important is discretion to you in a friend?

1   2   3   4   5   6   7   8   9   10

How important is a sense of style to you in a friend?

1   2   3   4   5   6   7   8   9   10

How important is affection to you in a friend?

1   2   3   4   5   6   7   8   9   10

How important is decisiveness to you in a friend?

1   2   3   4   5   6   7   8   9   10

How important is a sense of adventure to you in a friend?

1   2   3   4   5   6   7   8   9   10

# WHAT ARE YOUR THOUGHTS ON . . . ?

Genetically modified food?

_____

_____

_____

_____

Movie remakes?

_____

_____

_____

_____

Airline security?

_____

_____

_____

_____

Medicine?

_____

_____

_____

_____

## ASK SOMEONE

### THE NAME OF THE PERSON YOU'RE ASKING:

_____

In what part of the world do you imagine me being the happiest?

_____

What would you use to lure me into a trap?

_____

In a perfect world, who would I end up marrying?

_____

What is your favorite moment we've shared?

_____

What name do you think suits me better than my own?

_____

What things remind you of me?

_____

What do you hope I will always remember about you?

_____

# AT RANDOM

Someone you've always wanted to kiss:

_____

On my nightstand right now are these things:

_____

_____

_____

_____

_____

Skills I would like to learn are:

_____

_____

_____

_____

_____

Your favorite television channels are:

_____

_____

_____

_____

_____

# YOUR LISTS

Things that turn you on:

1. _____
2. _____
3. _____
4. _____
5. _____
6. _____
7. _____
8. _____

Things that turn you off:

1. _____
2. _____
3. _____
4. _____
5. _____
6. _____
7. _____
8. _____

Fictional characters who remind you of you:

1. _____

2. _____

3. _____

4. _____

5. _____

6. _____

7. _____

8. _____

9. _____


Celebrities whose style you admire:

1. _____

2. _____

3. _____

4. _____

5. _____

6. _____

7. _____

8. _____

9. _____

The first things you notice about someone you are attracted to:

1. _____
2. _____
3. _____
4. _____
5. _____

Your worst habits:

1. _____
2. _____
3. _____
4. _____
5. _____

Questions you hate being asked:

1. _____
2. _____
3. _____
4. _____
5. _____

"We have all a better guide in ourselves, if we would attend to it, than any other person can be."

—JANE AUSTEN, *Mansfield Park*

Right now I am thinking . . .

_____

_____

_____

_____

_____

_____

_____

_____

_____

# WHEN SOMEONE SAYS _____,
## YOU THINK . . .

Habit:

_____

Hammers:

_____

Hands:

_____

Help:

_____

Highway:

_____

Holes:

_____

Hope:

_____

Hours:

_____

House:

_____

Huge:

_____

Hungry:

_____

# TODAY I . . . LISTENED TO:

(LIST ALL OF THE MUSIC, PODCASTS,
OR RADIO SHOWS YOU LISTENED TO)

DATE: _____

1. _____

2. _____

3. _____

4. _____

5. _____

6. _____

7. _____

8. _____

9. _____

10. _____

11. _____

12. _____

13. _____

14. _____

15. _____

16. _____

# ARTIST FAVORITES

ARTIST NAME: _____

FAVORITE WORK OF ART: _____

_____

What do you love about this artist and this piece?

_____

_____

_____


ARTIST NAME: _____

FAVORITE WORK OF ART: _____

_____

What do you love about this artist and this piece?

_____

_____

_____


ARTIST NAME: _____

FAVORITE WORK OF ART: _____

_____

What do you love about this artist and this piece?

_____

_____

_____

ARTIST NAME: _____

FAVORITE WORK OF ART: _____

_____

What do you love about this artist and this piece?

_____

_____

_____


ARTIST NAME: _____

FAVORITE WORK OF ART: _____

_____

What do you love about this artist and this piece?

_____

_____

_____


ARTIST NAME: _____

FAVORITE WORK OF ART: _____

_____

What do you love about this artist and this piece?

_____

_____

_____

# YOUR LISTS

Elements of your dream home:

1. _____
2. _____
3. _____
4. _____
5. _____
6. _____
7. _____
8. _____


Strangest foods you tried:

1. _____
2. _____
3. _____
4. _____
5. _____
6. _____
7. _____
8. _____

Songs that remind you of your first love:

1. _____

2. _____

3. _____

4. _____

5. _____

6. _____

Songs you would want played at your wedding (or that you had played at your wedding):

1. _____

2. _____

3. _____

4. _____

5. _____

6. _____

Songs that make you want to jump up and dance:

1. _____

2. _____

3. _____

4. _____

5. _____

6. _____

Foods that are always on your grocery list:

1. _____
2. _____
3. _____
4. _____
5. _____
6. _____
7. _____
8. _____
9. _____
10. _____

Your favorite pizza toppings:

1. _____
2. _____
3. _____
4. _____
5. _____
6. _____
7. _____
8. _____
9. _____
10. _____

Belongings that are priceless for sentimental reasons:

1. _____
2. _____
3. _____
4. _____
5. _____
6. _____

Places you would never want to visit:

1. _____
2. _____
3. _____
4. _____
5. _____
6. _____

People you know who give the best hugs:

1. _____
2. _____
3. _____
4. _____
5. _____
6. _____

# AT RANDOM

If you could go back to school, what would you major in?

_____

Do you think you lived in a past life?
[  ] yes   [  ] no

If yes, when did you live and who do you think you
may have been?

_____

_____

Have you buried some sort of memorabilia in hopes someone
will discover it in the future?
[  ] yes   [  ] no

How many vehicles have you owned?

_____

List the makes and models:

_____

_____

_____

_____

_____

Do you believe in the Big Bang Theory?

[ ] yes [ ] no

Have you seen a UFO?

[ ] yes [ ] no

If yes, when and where?

_____

_____

Have you ridden a mechanical bull?

[ ] yes [ ] no

Have you been in or visited someone in jail?

[ ] yes [ ] no

Have you been to court?

[ ] yes [ ] no

Have you debated in front of a crowd?

[ ] yes [ ] no

Have you ever given a speech in front of a crowd?

[ ] yes [ ] no

If yes, when, where, and what about?

_____

_____

_____

# WHAT ARE YOUR THOUGHTS ON . . . ?

Texting?

_____

_____

_____

_____

Facial hair?

_____

_____

_____

_____

Preservatives?

_____

_____

_____

_____

Feng shui?

_____

_____

_____

_____

## ON A SCALE OF 1 TO 10

### (CIRCLE YOUR PREFERENCE)

How important is cautiousness to you in a friend?

1    2    3    4    5    6    7    8    9    10

How important is sensitivity to you in a friend?

1    2    3    4    5    6    7    8    9    10

How important is uniqueness to you in a friend?

1    2    3    4    5    6    7    8    9    10

How important is courtesy to you in a friend?

1    2    3    4    5    6    7    8    9    10

How important is intellectualism to you in a friend?

1    2    3    4    5    6    7    8    9    10

How important is flexibility to you in a friend?

1    2    3    4    5    6    7    8    9    10

How important are common interests to you in a friend?

1    2    3    4    5    6    7    8    9    10

How important is enjoyment of travel to you in a friend?

1    2    3    4    5    6    7    8    9    10

## THIS OR THAT
### (CIRCLE YOUR PREFERENCE)

Teddy bears OR Dolls

Mystery OR Understanding

Cocky OR Humble

Baby powder OR Baby oil

Caribbean cruise OR Arctic cruise

Cuddling OR Holding hands

Dentist visit OR Doctor visit

Table games OR Video games

Cotton candy OR Funnel cake

Volleyball OR Frisbee

Bottle OR Can

Gift wrap OR Gift bag

Dice OR Dominoes

Fix it yourself OR Pay someone to fix it

Drive OR Fly

Sarcasm OR Seriousness

Take a shower OR Take a bath

Zoos OR Aquariums

Public libraries OR Public parks

Cardio OR Weight training

Books OR Movies

Tennis shoes OR Flip-flops

Carpet OR Tile

Flowers OR Candy

Staples OR Paperclips

Indoor arena OR Outdoor stadium

High heels OR Flats

# SUPERSTITIONS

Do you believe crystals have magical properties?
[  ] yes  [  ] no

Do you believe the Yeti exists?
[  ] yes  [  ] no

Do you believe in numerology?
[  ] yes  [  ] no

Do you believe aliens had anything to do with the creation
of the Nazca Lines?
[  ] yes  [  ] no

Do you believe in palmistry?
[  ] yes  [  ] no

Would you take advice from a fortune-teller?
[  ] yes  [  ] no

Do you believe it's unlucky if two people say the same word
at the same time and don't immediately call it a jinx?
[  ] yes  [  ] no

Do you believe that when crossing railroad tracks
you should touch a screw for luck?
[  ] yes  [  ] no

Does the number "666" make you uncomfortable?
[  ] yes  [  ] no

When fishing, do you throw back your first catch, believing
it will make you more likely to continue catching fish?
[  ] yes  [  ] no

# YOUR LEAST FAVORITE

Breakfast food:

_____

Celebrity chef:

_____

Commercial jingle:

_____

Dessert:

_____

Foreign language:

_____

Hairstyle:

_____

Metal:

_____

Romantic film:

_____

Salad dressing:

_____

Shirt style:

_____

Valentine's Day gift:

_____

# YOUR MOST FAVORITE

Breakfast food:

_____

Celebrity chef:

_____

Commercial jingle:

_____

Dessert:

_____

Foreign language:

_____

Hairstyle:

_____

Metal:

_____

Romantic film:

_____

Salad dressing:

_____

Shirt style:

_____

Valentine's Day gift:

_____

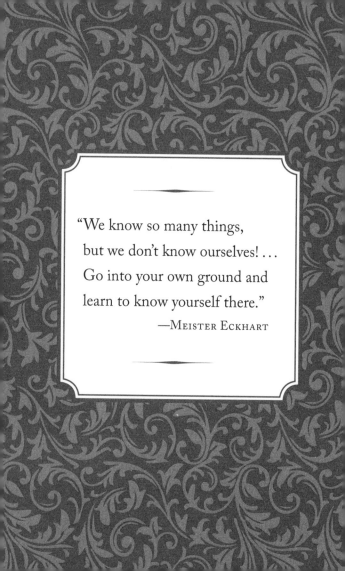

"We know so many things,
but we don't know ourselves! ...
Go into your own ground and
learn to know yourself there."

—MEISTER ECKHART

I am inspired by . . .

# YOUR LISTS

The best friends you've ever had:

1. _____
2. _____
3. _____
4. _____
5. _____
6. _____
7. _____
8. _____

Things you never thought you'd hear yourself say:

1. _____
2. _____
3. _____
4. _____
5. _____
6. _____
7. _____
8. _____

Your favorite guilty-pleasure television shows:

1. _____

2. _____

3. _____

4. _____

5. _____

6. _____

7. _____

8. _____

Your favorite guilty-pleasure books:

1. _____

2. _____

3. _____

4. _____

5. _____

6. _____

7. _____

8. _____

Television shows you'd like to appear on:

1. _____
2. _____
3. _____
4. _____
5. _____
6. _____

Nicknames you've given other people:

1. _____
2. _____
3. _____
4. _____
5. _____
6. _____

Things you'd like to do on a date:

1. _____
2. _____
3. _____
4. _____
5. _____
6. _____

Candies you like:

1. _____
2. _____
3. _____
4. _____
5. _____
6. _____

Candies you dislike:

1. _____
2. _____
3. _____
4. _____
5. _____
6. _____

Foreign words you think are sexy:

1. _____
2. _____
3. _____
4. _____
5. _____
6. _____

# TELEVISION FAVORITES:
# FAVORITE HEROES & HEROINES

SHOW TITLE: _____

CHARACTER NAME: _____

What makes this character heroic?

_____

_____


SHOW TITLE: _____

CHARACTER NAME: _____

What makes this character heroic?

_____

_____


SHOW TITLE: _____

CHARACTER NAME: _____

What makes this character heroic?

_____

_____


SHOW TITLE: _____

CHARACTER NAME: _____

What makes this character heroic?

_____

_____

# TELEVISION FAVORITES:
## VILLAINS

SHOW TITLE: _____

CHARACTER NAME: _____

What makes this character such a compelling villain?

_____

_____


SHOW TITLE: _____

CHARACTER NAME: _____

What makes this character such a compelling villain?

_____

_____


SHOW TITLE: _____

CHARACTER NAME: _____

What makes this character such a compelling villain?

_____

_____


SHOW TITLE: _____

CHARACTER NAME: _____

What makes this character such a compelling villain?

_____

_____

# TODAY I . . . BOUGHT:
### (LIST ALL OF THE THINGS YOU BOUGHT, AND WHERE)

DATE: _____

1. _____ at _____

2. _____ at _____

3. _____ at _____

4. _____ at _____

5. _____ at _____

6. _____ at _____

7. _____ at _____

8. _____ at _____

9. _____ at _____

10. _____ at _____

11. _____ at _____

12. _____ at _____

13. _____ at _____

14. _____ at _____

15. _____ at _____

## WHEN SOMEONE SAYS _____,
## YOU THINK . . .

Ice:
_____

Iffy:
_____

Incredible:
_____

Ink:
_____

Impossible:
_____

Insecure :
_____

Infection:
_____

Iridescent:
_____

Iron:
_____

Irregular:
_____

Itch:
_____

# AT RANDOM

If you were a rapper, you'd go by what name?

_____

How do you prefer your steaks cooked?

_____

The most memorable untrue rumor ever spread about you:

_____

A party isn't a party until:

_____

_____

Would you bring dinosaurs back from extinction
if you could?

[ ] yes  [ ] no

When a telemarketer calls and you happen to answer the
phone, what do you usually do?

_____

_____

If you could've chosen your name, it would be:

_____

Something people make fun of you for:

_____

_____

Something people praise you for:

_____

_____

You would say you behave mostly like which of your parents?

_____

The most joy you ever derived from working:

_____

_____

The least joy you ever derived from working:

_____

_____

Which of your parents do you resemble the most?

_____

Did you ever skip school?

[   ] yes   [   ] no

If you have children do they live with you?

[   ] yes   [   ] no

# SUPERSTITIONS

Would you feel uneasy getting out of bed left foot first?
[ ] yes [ ] no

Do you believe trees are conscious?
[ ] yes [ ] no

Does seeing cows lying down in a field make you think
it's going to rain?
[ ] yes [ ] no

Do you believe vampires ever existed?
[ ] yes [ ] no

Do you believe aliens had anything to do with the statues
found on Easter Island?
[ ] yes [ ] no

Do you believe it's unlucky to see your face in a mirror
by candlelight?
[ ] yes [ ] no

Do you believe it's unlucky to send Christmas carolers
away empty-handed?
[ ] yes [ ] no

Do you believe lightning never strikes twice?
[ ] yes [ ] no

Do you believe salty soup is a sign that the cook is in love?
[ ] yes [ ] no

# WHAT ARE YOUR THOUGHTS ON . . . ?

Professional wrestling?

_____

_____

_____

_____

Instant messaging?

_____

_____

_____

_____

E-mail?

_____

_____

_____

_____

Voicemail?

_____

_____

_____

_____

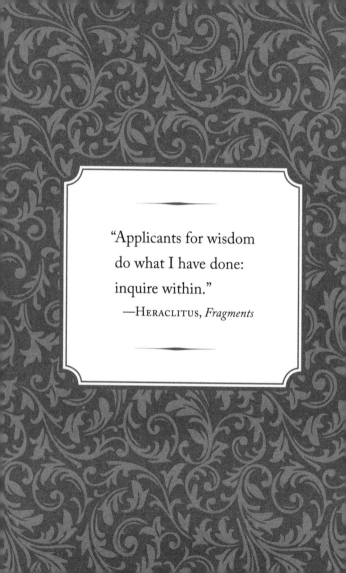

"Applicants for wisdom
do what I have done:
inquire within."
—HERACLITUS, *Fragments*

I am happy because . . .

_____
_____
_____
_____
_____
_____
_____
_____
_____

# YOUR LISTS

Your ideal dinner party guests, from any time in history:

1. _____
2. _____
3. _____
4. _____
5. _____
6. _____
7. _____
8. _____

The worst movies ever made in your opinion:

1. _____
2. _____
3. _____
4. _____
5. _____
6. _____
7. _____
8. _____

Weddings you've attended:

1. _____
2. _____
3. _____
4. _____
5. _____
6. _____
7. _____
8. _____

Graduations you've attended:

1. _____
2. _____
3. _____
4. _____
5. _____
6. _____
7. _____
8. _____

Things you do directly after waking up:

1. _____
2. _____
3. _____
4. _____
5. _____
6. _____
7. _____
8. _____
9. _____

Things you do directly before you go to bed:

1. _____
2. _____
3. _____
4. _____
5. _____
6. _____
7. _____
8. _____
9. _____

Songs on your playlist right now:

PLAYLIST NAME: _____

1. _____
2. _____
3. _____
4. _____
5. _____
6. _____
7. _____
8. _____
9. _____
10. _____
11. _____
12. _____
13. _____
14. _____
15. _____
16. _____
17. _____
18. _____

# TODAY I . . . ACCOMPLISHED THESE THINGS ON MY TO-DO LIST:

DATE: _____

1. _____
2. _____
3. _____
4. _____
5. _____
6. _____
7. _____
8. _____

# . . . BUT I DID NOT HAVE TIME TO DO:

1. _____
2. _____
3. _____
4. _____
5. _____
6. _____
7. _____
8. _____

# ON A SCALE OF 1 TO 10

## (CIRCLE YOUR PREFERENCE)

How important are street smarts to you in a life partner?

1    2    3    4    5    6    7    8    9    10

How important is gracefulness to you in a life partner?

1    2    3    4    5    6    7    8    9    10

How important is edginess to you in a life partner?

1    2    3    4    5    6    7    8    9    10

How important is a good kissing technique to you in a life partner?

1    2    3    4    5    6    7    8    9    10

How important is self-control to you in a life partner?

1    2    3    4    5    6    7    8    9    10

How important is a good work ethic to you in a life partner?

1    2    3    4    5    6    7    8    9    10

How important is having good business sense and financial acumen to you in a life partner?

1    2    3    4    5    6    7    8    9    10

How important is the ability to communicate to you in a life partner?

1    2    3    4    5    6    7    8    9    10

How important is inner beauty to you in a life partner?

1    2    3    4    5    6    7    8    9    10

How important is a love of family to you in a life partner?

1    2    3    4    5    6    7    8    9    10

# WHEN SOMEONE SAYS _____,
## YOU THINK . . .

Jacket:

_____

Jaded:

_____

Jam:

_____

January:

_____

Jasmine:

_____

Jealous:

_____

Jet lag:

_____

Jittery:

_____

Jolly:

_____

Joy:

_____

Junk:

_____

# TELEVISION FAVORITES:
# CLASSIC COMEDIES

SHOW TITLE: _____

EPISODE/SEASON: _____

What was so funny about this show?

_____

_____


SHOW TITLE: _____

EPISODE/SEASON: _____

What was so funny about this show?

_____

_____


SHOW TITLE: _____

EPISODE/SEASON: _____

What was so funny about this show?

_____

_____


SHOW TITLE: _____

EPISODE/SEASON: _____

What was so funny about this show?

_____

_____

# TELEVISION FAVORITES:
## MODERN COMEDIES

SHOW TITLE: _____

EPISODE/SEASON: _____

What was so funny about this show?

_____

_____


SHOW TITLE: _____

EPISODE/SEASON: _____

What was so funny about this show?

_____

_____


SHOW TITLE: _____

EPISODE/SEASON: _____

What was so funny about this show?

_____

_____


SHOW TITLE: _____

EPISODE/SEASON: _____

What was so funny about this show?

_____

_____

# AT RANDOM

Do you sing in the shower?
[ ] yes  [ ] no

Have you dated two or more people with the same first name?
[ ] yes  [ ] no

Do you have a birthmark?
[ ] yes  [ ] no

Have you waxed any part of your body?
[ ] yes  [ ] no

Have you used the sun to reference your direction?
[ ] yes  [ ] no

Have you been on an airplane over the ocean?
[ ] yes  [ ] no

Do you have a good sense of smell?
[ ] yes  [ ] no

Sports you have played, and if on a team, your position:

_____

_____

_____

_____

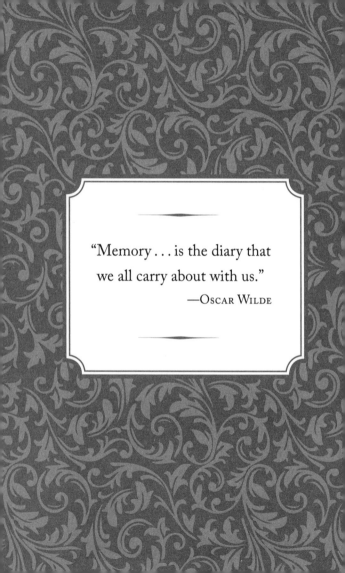

"Memory . . . is the diary that
we all carry about with us."

—Oscar Wilde

Right now I am thinking . . .

# YOUR LISTS

Words that best describe your father:

1. _____
2. _____
3. _____
4. _____
5. _____
6. _____
7. _____
8. _____

Words that best describe your mother:

1. _____
2. _____
3. _____
4. _____
5. _____
6. _____
7. _____
8. _____

Ways your life differs from your parents' lives:

1. _____
2. _____
3. _____
4. _____
5. _____
6. _____

Holidays you like:

1. _____
2. _____
3. _____
4. _____
5. _____
6. _____

Holidays you dislike:

1. _____
2. _____
3. _____
4. _____
5. _____
6. _____

Traditional holiday meals your family makes,
and for what holiday:

1. _____

   for _____

2. _____

   for _____

3. _____

   for _____

4. _____

   for _____

5. _____

   for _____

6. _____

   for _____

7. _____

   for _____

8. _____

   for _____

9. _____

   for _____

10. _____

   for _____

11. _____

   for _____

Your top four most memorable holidays, and why:

1. _____

   _____

   _____

   _____

2. _____

   _____

   _____

   _____

   _____

3. _____

   _____

   _____

   _____

   _____

4. _____

   _____

   _____

   _____

   _____

# TODAY I . . . VISITED THESE WEBSITES:

(LIST ALL OF THE SITES YOU SURFED TODAY, ALONG WITH
WHAT YOU LOOKED AT OR READ ON THOSE SITES)

DATE: _____

1. _____
   to find _____

2. _____
   to find _____

3. _____
   to find _____

4. _____
   to find _____

5. _____
   to find _____

6. _____
   to find _____

7. _____
   to find _____

8. _____
   to find _____

9. _____
   to find _____

10. _____
   to find _____

11. _____
   to find _____

## WHEN SOMEONE SAYS _____,
## YOU THINK ...

Kale:

_____

Keepsake:

_____

Keys:

_____

Kitchen:

_____

Kittens:

_____

Kites:

_____

Klutzy:

_____

Knocking:

_____

Knowledge:

_____

Kooky:

_____

Kudos:

_____

# FILM FAVORITES:
## FAVORITE HEROES & HEROINES

FILM TITLE: _____

CHARACTER NAME: _____

What makes this character heroic?

_____

_____


FILM TITLE: _____

CHARACTER NAME: _____

What makes this character heroic?

_____

_____


FILM TITLE: _____

CHARACTER NAME: _____

What makes this character heroic?

_____

_____


FILM TITLE: _____

CHARACTER NAME: _____

What makes this character heroic?

_____

_____

# FILM FAVORITES:
## VILLAINS

FILM TITLE: _____

CHARACTER NAME: _____

What makes this character such a compelling villain?

_____

_____


FILM TITLE: _____

CHARACTER NAME: _____

What makes this character such a compelling villain?

_____

_____


FILM TITLE: _____

CHARACTER NAME: _____

What makes this character such a compelling villain?

_____

_____


FILM TITLE: _____

CHARACTER NAME: _____

What makes this character such a compelling villain?

_____

_____

# AT RANDOM

Do you attend religious services?
[ ] yes   [ ] no

If yes, how often?

_____

Have you gone to jury duty?
[ ] yes   [ ] no

If yes, did you ever sit on a jury in an actual trial?
[ ] yes   [ ] no

Your favorite cheeses:

_____
_____
_____
_____
_____

Your least-favorite cheeses:

_____
_____
_____
_____
_____

# YOUR LISTS

Your greatest strengths:

1. _____
2. _____
3. _____
4. _____
5. _____
6. _____
7. _____
8. _____

Your greatest weaknesses:

1. _____
2. _____
3. _____
4. _____
5. _____
6. _____
7. _____
8. _____

Things you have no interest in learning:

1. _____
2. _____
3. _____
4. _____
5. _____
6. _____

Voices you find sexy:

1. _____
2. _____
3. _____
4. _____
5. _____
6. _____

Voices you find irritating:

1. _____
2. _____
3. _____
4. _____
5. _____
6. _____

Smells you like:

1. _____
2. _____
3. _____
4. _____
5. _____
7. _____
8. _____
9. _____
10. _____

Smells you dislike:

1. _____
2. _____
3. _____
4. _____
5. _____
7. _____
8. _____
9. _____
10. _____

# TODODAY I . . . COOKED:
### (LIST THE DISHES YOU COOKED TODAY OR
### MEALS YOU PREPARED, AND THEIR MAIN INGREDIENTS)

DATE: _____

**DISH 1:**

_____

**INGREDIENTS:**

1. _____

2. _____

3. _____

**DISH 2:**

_____

**INGREDIENTS:**

1. _____

2. _____

3. _____

**DISH 3:**

_____

**INGREDIENTS:**

1. _____

2. _____

3. _____

# WHAT ARE YOUR THOUGHTS ON . . . ?

Sex appeal?

_____

_____

_____

_____

Bottled water?

_____

_____

_____

_____

Animal intelligence?

_____

_____

_____

_____

Raw food diet?

_____

_____

_____

_____

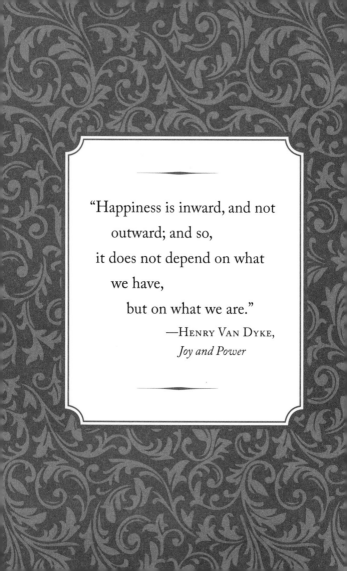

"Happiness is inward, and not outward; and so,
it does not depend on what we have,
but on what we are."

—HENRY VAN DYKE,
*Joy and Power*

I am inspired by . . .

# WHEN SOMEONE SAYS _____,
## YOU THINK . . .

Lace:

_____

Lakes:

_____

Laughter:

_____

Late:

_____

Lazy:

_____

Leader:

_____

Lights:

_____

Lightning:

_____

Locks:

_____

Love:

_____

Lust:

_____

# AT RANDOM

Were you ever in a book club?

[ ] yes   [ ] no

Were you or are you a member in any other type of club?

[ ] yes   [ ] no

If yes, list the clubs:

_____

_____

_____

_____

How do you get around town?

____ Bicycle        ____ Rollerblades

____ Bus            ____ Skateboard

____ Car or van     ____ Subway

____ Moped          ____ Train

____ Motorcycle     ____ Walk

If you can drink, your favorite alcoholic beverages are:

_____

_____

_____

_____

_____

# MORE FILM FAVORITES:
## CLASSIC COMEDIES

FILM NAME: _____

FAVORITE CHARACTER: _____

WHERE DID YOU SEE IT? _____

WHO DID YOU SEE IT WITH? _____

What was the funniest scene in the film?

_____


FILM NAME: _____

FAVORITE CHARACTER: _____

WHERE DID YOU SEE IT? _____

WHO DID YOU SEE IT WITH? _____

What was the funniest scene in the film?

_____


FILM NAME: _____

FAVORITE CHARACTER: _____

WHERE DID YOU SEE IT? _____

WHO DID YOU SEE IT WITH? _____

What was the funniest scene in the film?

_____

# MORE FILM FAVORITES:
## MODERN COMEDIES

FILM NAME: _____

FAVORITE CHARACTER: _____

WHERE DID YOU SEE IT? _____

WHO DID YOU SEE IT WITH? _____

What was the funniest scene in the film?

_____


FILM NAME: _____

FAVORITE CHARACTER: _____

WHERE DID YOU SEE IT? _____

WHO DID YOU SEE IT WITH? _____

What was the funniest scene in the film?

_____


FILM NAME: _____

FAVORITE CHARACTER: _____

WHERE DID YOU SEE IT? _____

WHO DID YOU SEE IT WITH? _____

What was the funniest scene in the film?

_____

# YOUR LISTS

Childhood meals you loved:

1. _____
2. _____
3. _____
4. _____
5. _____
6. _____
7. _____
8. _____

Quotes and phrases you like or often say:

1. _____
2. _____
3. _____
4. _____
5. _____
6. _____
7. _____
8. _____

Colors you like:

1. _____
2. _____
3. _____
4. _____
5. _____
6. _____
7. _____
8. _____

Colors you dislike or tend to avoid:

1. _____
2. _____
3. _____
4. _____
5. _____
6. _____
7. _____
8. _____

Things you'd enjoy about being famous:

1. _____
2. _____
3. _____
4. _____
5. _____
6. _____
7. _____
8. _____
9. _____

Things you'd dislike about being famous:

1. _____
2. _____
3. _____
4. _____
5. _____
6. _____
7. _____
8. _____
9. _____

Songs on your playlist right now:

PLAYLIST NAME: _____

1. _____
2. _____
3. _____
4. _____
5. _____
6. _____
7. _____
8. _____
9. _____
10. _____
11. _____
12. _____
13. _____
14. _____
15. _____
16. _____
17. _____
18. _____

# TODODAY I . . . SPOKE TO:

(LIST ALL OF THE PEOPLE YOU EXCHANGED
WORDS WITH TODAY)

DATE: _____

1. _____
2. _____
3. _____
4. _____
5. _____
6. _____
7. _____
8. _____
9. _____
10. _____
11. _____
12. _____
13. _____
14. _____
15. _____
16. _____

# ASK SOMEONE

## THE NAME OF THE PERSON YOU'RE ASKING:

_____

In what part of the world do you imagine me being the happiest?

_____

What would you use to lure me into a trap?

_____

In a perfect world, who would I end up marrying?

_____

What is your favorite moment we've shared?

_____

What name do you think suits me better than my own?

_____

What things remind you of me?

_____

What do you hope I will always remember about you?

_____

## ON A SCALE OF 1 TO 10

### (CIRCLE YOUR PREFERENCE)

How important are street smarts to you in a friend?

1   2   3   4   5   6   7   8   9   10

How important is gracefulness to you in a friend?

1   2   3   4   5   6   7   8   9   10

How important is edginess to you in a friend?

1   2   3   4   5   6   7   8   9   10

How important is athleticism to you in a friend?

1   2   3   4   5   6   7   8   9   10

How important is self-control to you in a friend?

1   2   3   4   5   6   7   8   9   10

How important is a good work ethic to you in a friend?

1   2   3   4   5   6   7   8   9   10

How important is having good business sense and financial acumen to you in a friend?

1   2   3   4   5   6   7   8   9   10

How important is the ability to communicate to you in a friend?

1   2   3   4   5   6   7   8   9   10

How important is inner beauty to you in a friend?

1   2   3   4   5   6   7   8   9   10

How important is a love of family to you in a friend?

1   2   3   4   5   6   7   8   9   10

# WHAT ARE YOUR THOUGHTS ON . . . ?

Cable television?

_____

_____

_____

_____

Paleo diets?

_____

_____

_____

_____

Juicing?

_____

_____

_____

_____

Public polls?

_____

_____

_____

_____

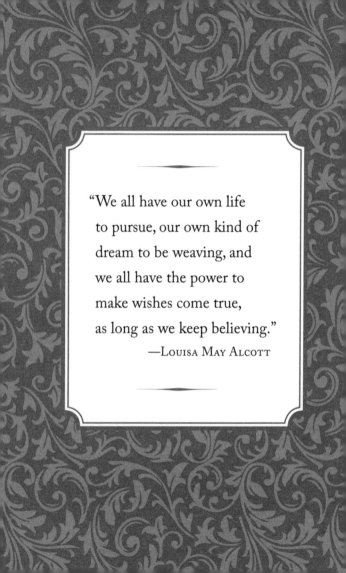

"We all have our own life to pursue, our own kind of dream to be weaving, and we all have the power to make wishes come true, as long as we keep believing."

—Louisa May Alcott

I am happy because . . .

## WHEN SOMEONE SAYS _____,
## YOU THINK . . .

Magic:

_____

Majestic:

_____

Makeup:

_____

Masks:

_____

Mentor:

_____

Mermaids:

_____

Milk:

_____

Moonlight:

_____

Mountains:

_____

Morals:

_____

Mud:

_____

# AT RANDOM

Languages you are fluent in:

_____

_____

_____

Which continents have you been on?
____ Atlantic    ____ Southern    ____ Pacific
____ Arctic      ____ Indian

Which oceans have you seen in person?
____ Africa           ____ Europe        ____ Antarctica
____ North America    ____ Asia          ____ South America
____ Australia

Cuisines you have tried:
____ Central African    ____ Argentine      ____ Belgian/Dutch
____ Brazilian          ____ British        ____ Cajun
____ Chinese            ____ East African   ____ French
____ German/Austrian    ____ Greek          ____ Hungarian
____ Indian             ____ Irish          ____ Italian
____ Japanese           ____ Jewish         ____ Korean
____ Malaysian          ____ Mexican        ____ Middle Eastern
____ New England (U.S.) ____ North African  ____ Oceanic
____ Pakistani          ____ Polish         ____ Portuguese
____ Russian            ____ Scandinavian   ____ Scottish
____ South African      ____ Southern (U.S.)____ Southwestern (U.S.)
____ Spanish            ____ Swiss          ____ Thai
____ Turkish            ____ Vietnamese

# MORE BOOK FAVORITES:
## MODERN MASTERS

BOOK TITLE: _____

AUTHOR: _____

FAVORITE CHARACTER: _____

FAVORITE SCENE: _____

What did you like about this book?

_____

_____


BOOK TITLE: _____

AUTHOR: _____

FAVORITE CHARACTER: _____

FAVORITE SCENE: _____

What did you like about this book?

_____

_____


BOOK TITLE: _____

AUTHOR: _____

FAVORITE CHARACTER: _____

FAVORITE SCENE: _____

What did you like about this book?

_____

_____

BOOK TITLE: _____

AUTHOR: _____

FAVORITE CHARACTER: _____

FAVORITE SCENE: _____

What did you like about this book?

_____

_____

BOOK TITLE: _____

AUTHOR: _____

FAVORITE CHARACTER: _____

FAVORITE SCENE: _____

What did you like about this book?

_____

_____

BOOK TITLE: _____

AUTHOR: _____

FAVORITE CHARACTER: _____

FAVORITE SCENE: _____

What did you like about this book?

_____

_____

# YOUR LISTS

Things that remind you of winter:

1. _____

2. _____

3. _____

4. _____

5. _____

6. _____

7. _____

8. _____

Things that remind you of spring:

1. _____

2. _____

3. _____

4. _____

5. _____

6. _____

7. _____

8. _____

Things that remind you of summer:

1. _____

2. _____

3. _____

4. _____

5. _____

6. _____

7. _____

8. _____

Things that remind you of autumn:

1. _____

2. _____

3. _____

4. _____

5. _____

6. _____

7. _____

8. _____

Musicians you're attracted to:

1. _____
2. _____
3. _____
4. _____
5. _____
6. _____

Musicians you wish were still making music:

1. _____
2. _____
3. _____
4. _____
5. _____
6. _____

Musicians you think should stop making music:

1. _____
2. _____
3. _____
4. _____
5. _____
6. _____

Historical buildings or monuments you've visited:

1. _____
2. _____
3. _____
4. _____
5. _____
6. _____
7. _____
8. _____
9. _____


Incredible nature sites or natural wonders you've visited:

1. _____
2. _____
3. _____
4. _____
5. _____
6. _____
7. _____
8. _____
9. _____

# TODAY I . . . WENT TO:

(LIST ALL OF THE PLACES YOU WENT TODAY)

DATE: _____

1. _____
2. _____
3. _____
4. _____
5. _____
6. _____
7. _____
8. _____
9. _____
10. _____
11. _____
12. _____
13. _____
14. _____
15. _____
16. _____

# THIS OR THAT
(CIRCLE YOUR PREFERENCE)

Brick homes OR Log cabins

Cinnamon OR Mint

Road trips OR Cruises

Lemons OR Limes

Bowling OR Golfing

Popularity OR Knowledge

Pills OR Liquid medications

Gymnastics OR Figure skating

Convenience OR Challenge

Tinted windows OR Non-tinted windows

Oil paintings OR Watercolor paintings

Fireworks OR Laser light shows

Mailing address OR P.O. Box

Odd OR Even

Philosophy OR Psychology

Headset OR Handset

Butterflies OR Ladybugs

Towel OR Robe

Being tactful OR Being blunt

Hills OR Plains

Marble OR Steel

Horse races OR Car races

Old favorite OR Next big thing

Highways OR Rural roads

Delivery OR Takeout

Rent OR Buy

Air conditioning OR Fan

"Life can only be understood backwards; but it must be lived forwards."

—Søren Kierkegaard

Right now I am thinking . . .

_____

_____

_____

_____

_____

_____

_____

_____

_____

# WHEN SOMEONE SAYS _____,
## YOU THINK . . .

Naive:

_____

Naps:

_____

Natural:

_____

Needs:

_____

Negativity:

_____

Nervous:

_____

Nicest:

_____

Nightmares:

_____

Nonsense:

_____

Nourishing:

_____

Nurse:

_____

# YOUR LISTS

Things you like to touch:

1. _____
2. _____
3. _____
4. _____
5. _____
6. _____
7. _____
8. _____

Things you don't like to touch:

1. _____
2. _____
3. _____
4. _____
5. _____
6. _____
7. _____
8. _____

Things you like to see:

1. _____
2. _____
3. _____
4. _____
5. _____
6. _____
7. _____
8. _____
9. _____

Things you don't like to see:

1. _____
2. _____
3. _____
4. _____
5. _____
6. _____
7. _____
8. _____
9. _____

People you think would make a great president:

1. _____

2. _____

3. _____

4. _____

5. _____

6. _____

The world's worst inventions:

1. _____

2. _____

3. _____

4. _____

5. _____

6. _____

The strangest things you've placed on a to-do list:

1. _____

2. _____

3. _____

4. _____

5. _____

6. _____

Songs on your playlist right now:

PLAYLIST NAME: _____

1. _____

2. _____

3. _____

4. _____

5. _____

6. _____

7. _____

8. _____

9. _____

10. _____

11. _____

12. _____

13. _____

14. _____

15. _____

16. _____

17. _____

18. _____

# WHAT ARE YOUR THOUGHTS ON . . . ?

Political campaigns?

_____

_____

_____

_____

Artificial intelligence?

_____

_____

_____

_____

Tipping?

_____

_____

_____

STEM (science, technology, engineering, math) studies?

_____

_____

_____

_____

# MORE MUSIC FAVORITES:
## CONTEMPORARY
(LIST YOUR FAVORITE NEW ARTISTS AND SONGS
FROM THE PAST YEAR)

ARTIST NAME: _____

ALBUM: _____

SONG: _____

What do you find catchy about this song?

_____

_____


ARTIST NAME: _____

ALBUM: _____

SONG: _____

What do you find catchy about this song?

_____

_____


ARTIST NAME: _____

ALBUM: _____

SONG: _____

What do you find catchy about this song?

_____

_____

ARTIST NAME: _____

ALBUM: _____

SONG: _____

What do you find catchy about this song?

_____

_____

ARTIST NAME: _____

ALBUM: _____

SONG: _____

What do you find catchy about this song?

_____

_____

ARTIST NAME: _____

ALBUM: _____

SONG: _____

What do you find catchy about this song?

_____

_____

ARTIST NAME: _____

ALBUM: _____

SONG: _____

What do you find catchy about this song?

_____

_____

# TODAY I . . . WATCHED:

(LIST ALL OF THE VIDEOS, SHOWS, OR MOVIES YOU
WATCHED ONLINE, STREAMING, ON TV, OR AT A CINEMA)

DATE: _____

1. _____
2. _____
3. _____
4. _____
5. _____
6. _____
7. _____
8. _____
9. _____
10. _____
11. _____
12. _____
13. _____
14. _____
15. _____
16. _____

# WHEN SOMEONE SAYS _____,
## YOU THINK . . .

Obsessed:

_____

Obvious:

_____

Offense:

_____

Open:

_____

Ornaments:

_____

Passion:

_____

Perfection:

_____

Polite:

_____

Positivity:

_____

Pride:

_____

Propaganda:

_____

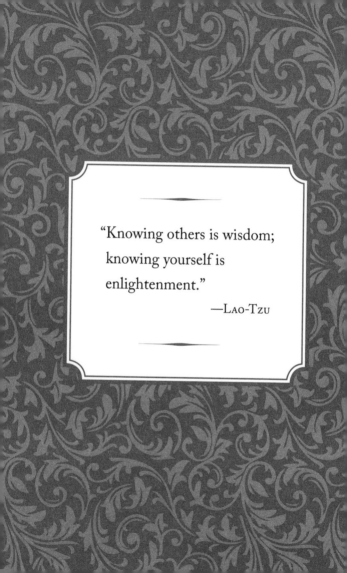

"Knowing others is wisdom;
knowing yourself is
enlightenment."

—Lao-Tzu

Right now I am thinking . . .

# YOUR LISTS

Things you like to do on your day off:

1. _____
2. _____
3. _____
4. _____
5. _____
6. _____
7. _____
8. _____

Things that make a good parent:

1. _____
2. _____
3. _____
4. _____
5. _____
6. _____
7. _____
8. _____

The coolest street names you've encountered:

1. _____
2. _____
3. _____
4. _____
5. _____
6. _____

Things you are saving up for:

1. _____
2. _____
3. _____
4. _____
5. _____
6. _____

Your current hobbies:

1. _____
2. _____
3. _____
4. _____
5. _____
6. _____

Museums you like:

1. _____
2. _____
3. _____
4. _____
5. _____
6. _____
7. _____
8. _____
9. _____
10. _____

Online videos or video series you like:

1. _____
2. _____
3. _____
4. _____
5. _____
6. _____
7. _____
8. _____
9. _____
10. _____

Things you don't miss about being a child:

1. _____

2. _____

3. _____

4. _____

5. _____

6. _____

Things you hate that others seem to love:

1. _____

2. _____

3. _____

4. _____

5. _____

6. _____

Things you keep in boxes:

1. _____

2. _____

3. _____

4. _____

5. _____

6. _____

# AT RANDOM

Have you ever revisited your childhood home?

_____

The best relationship advice you could give someone:

_____

_____

_____

_____

Who was your favorite babysitter?

_____

Did you ever babysit someone outside your siblings?
[ ] yes   [ ] no

Who?

_____

_____

Have you searched for yourself online?
[ ] yes   [ ] no

Have you searched for an old friend or love interest online?
[ ] yes   [ ] no

## WHEN SOMEONE SAYS _____,
## YOU THINK . . .

Quagmire:

_____

Qualified:

_____

Quality:

_____

Queen:

_____

Quenching:

_____

Quest:

_____

Quiet:

_____

Quilts:

_____

Quirky:

_____

Quickly:

_____

Quotes:

_____

# MORE FILM FAVORITES: CLASSIC SCI-FI

FILM NAME: _____

FAVORITE CHARACTER: _____

WHERE DID YOU SEE IT? _____

WHO DID YOU SEE IT WITH? _____

What did you like about this film?

_____


FILM NAME: _____

FAVORITE CHARACTER: _____

WHERE DID YOU SEE IT? _____

WHO DID YOU SEE IT WITH? _____

What did you like about this film?

_____


FILM NAME: _____

FAVORITE CHARACTER: _____

WHERE DID YOU SEE IT? _____

WHO DID YOU SEE IT WITH? _____

What did you like about this film?

_____

# MORE FILM FAVORITES: MODERN SCI-FI

FILM NAME: _____

FAVORITE CHARACTER: _____

WHERE DID YOU SEE IT? _____

WHO DID YOU SEE IT WITH? _____

What did you like about this film?

_____


FILM NAME: _____

FAVORITE CHARACTER: _____

WHERE DID YOU SEE IT? _____

WHO DID YOU SEE IT WITH? _____

What did you like about this film?

_____


FILM NAME: _____

FAVORITE CHARACTER: _____

WHERE DID YOU SEE IT? _____

WHO DID YOU SEE IT WITH? _____

What did you like about this film?

_____

# TODAY I . . . VISITED THESE WEBSITES:

(LIST ALL OF THE SITES YOU SURFED TODAY, ALONG WITH
WHAT YOU LOOKED AT OR READ ON THOSE SITES)

DATE: _____

1. _____

   to find _____

2. _____

   to find _____

3. _____

   to find _____

4. _____

   to find _____

5. _____

   to find _____

6. _____

   to find _____

7. _____

   to find _____

8. _____

   to find _____

9. _____

   to find _____

10. _____

   to find _____

11. _____

   to find _____

## ON A SCALE OF 1 TO 10
### (CIRCLE YOUR PREFERENCE)

How important to you is courage in a life partner?

1   2   3   4   5   6   7   8   9   10

How important are writing skills to you in a life partner?

1   2   3   4   5   6   7   8   9   10

How important is having a good design sense to you in a life partner?

1   2   3   4   5   6   7   8   9   10

How important is a pleasing voice to you in a life partner?

1   2   3   4   5   6   7   8   9   10

How important are good cooking skills to you in a life partner?

1   2   3   4   5   6   7   8   9   10

How important is it to you that your life partner does not smoke?

1   2   3   4   5   6   7   8   9   10

How important is it to you that your life partner does not drink?

1   2   3   4   5   6   7   8   9   10

How important to you is health-consciousness in a life partner?

1   2   3   4   5   6   7   8   9   10

How important is environmental awareness to you in a
life partner?

1   2   3   4   5   6   7   8   9   10

How important is an outgoing personality to you in a life partner?

1   2   3   4   5   6   7   8   9   10

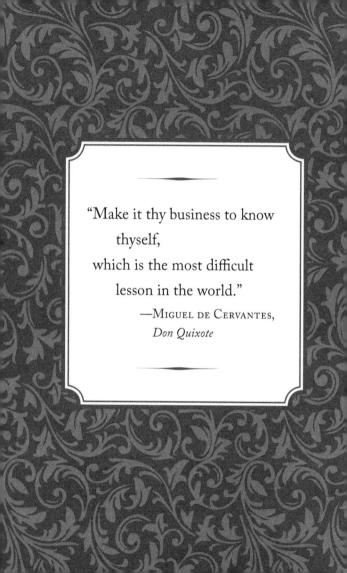

"Make it thy business to know thyself,
which is the most difficult
lesson in the world."

—MIGUEL DE CERVANTES,
*Don Quixote*

I am inspired by . . .

# WHEN SOMEONE SAYS _____,
## YOU THINK . . .

Racket:

_____

Rain:

_____

Rainbows:

_____

Regret:

_____

Relief:

_____

Ridiculous:

_____

Rings:

_____

Rivers:

_____

Rocky:

_____

Rude:

_____

Rules:

_____

# YOUR LISTS

Your favorite poems:

1. _____

2. _____

3. _____

4. _____

5. _____

6. _____

7. _____

8. _____

Your favorite animals:

. _____

2. _____

3. _____

4. _____

5. _____

6. _____

7. _____

8. _____

Restaurants you frequently go to:

1. _____

2. _____

3. _____

4. _____

5. _____

6. _____


Dishes you like to take out:

1. _____

2. _____

3. _____

4. _____

5. _____

6. _____


Dishes you like to order in:

1. _____

2. _____

3. _____

4. _____

5. _____

6. _____

Stores you frequently shop at:

1. _____
2. _____
3. _____
4. _____
5. _____
6. _____
7. _____
8. _____
9. _____
10. _____

Stores you would like to shop in one day:

1. _____
2. _____
3. _____
4. _____
5. _____
6. _____
7. _____
8. _____
9. _____
10. _____

Things you do not fear, which scare other people:

1. _____

2. _____

3. _____

4. _____

5. _____

6. _____


Scariest movies you've seen:

1. _____

2. _____

3. _____

4. _____

5. _____

6. _____


Scariest books you've read:

1. _____

2. _____

3. _____

4. _____

5. _____

6. _____

# AT RANDOM

Your longest drive—how many hours and to where?

_____

_____


The most spiritual place you have ever been:

_____

_____

_____


Do you cry at sentimental movies or shows?

[ ] yes   [ ] no


Have you ever been in a cave?

[ ] yes   [ ] no


Have you ever been camping?

[ ] yes   [ ] no

If yes, where?

_____

_____


Have you ever participated in a science fair?

[ ] yes   [ ] no

## TODAY I . . . BOUGHT:
### (LIST ALL OF THE THINGS YOU BOUGHT, AND WHERE)

DATE: _____

1. _____ at _____

2. _____ at _____

3. _____ at _____

4. _____ at _____

5. _____ at _____

6. _____ at _____

7. _____ at _____

8. _____ at _____

9. _____ at _____

10. _____ at _____

11. _____ at _____

12. _____ at _____

13. _____ at _____

14. _____ at _____

15. _____ at _____

## WHEN SOMEONE SAYS _____,
## YOU THINK . . .

Sand:

_____

Satiny:

_____

Screens:

_____

Seeds:

_____

Shadows:

_____

Sleep:

_____

Snow:

_____

Soap:

_____

Stairs:

_____

Sticky:

_____

Sultry:

_____

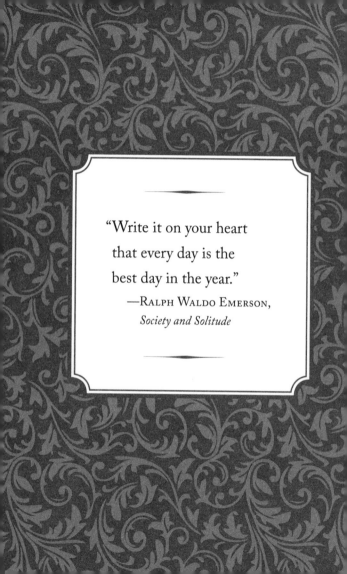

"Write it on your heart
that every day is the
best day in the year."
—Ralph Waldo Emerson,
*Society and Solitude*

I am happy because . . .

_____

_____

_____

_____

_____

_____

_____

_____

_____

# YOUR LISTS

People who were big influences on you:

1. _____

2. _____

3. _____

4. _____

5. _____

6. _____

7. _____

8. _____


Jobs you have had:

1. _____

2. _____

3. _____

4. _____

5. _____

6. _____

7. _____

8. _____

The best bosses or supervisors you have had:

1. _____
2. _____
3. _____
4. _____
5. _____
6. _____

The worst bosses or supervisors you have had:

1. _____
2. _____
3. _____
4. _____
5. _____
6. _____

Good friends you made at a job:

1. _____
2. _____
3. _____
4. _____
5. _____
6. _____

Sounds you like:

1. _____

2. _____

3. _____

4. _____

5. _____

6. _____

7. _____

8. _____

9. _____

Sounds you dislike:

1. _____

2. _____

3. _____

4. _____

5. _____

6. _____

7. _____

8. _____

9. _____

Songs on your playlist right now:

PLAYLIST NAME: _____

1. _____
2. _____
3. _____
4. _____
5. _____
6. _____
7. _____
8. _____
9. _____
10. _____
11. _____
12. _____
13. _____
14. _____
15. _____
16. _____
17. _____
18. _____

# MORE BOOK FAVORITES:
## FAVORITE HEROES & HEROINES

BOOK TITLE: _____

AUTHOR: _____

FAVORITE CHARACTER: _____

FAVORITE SCENE: _____

What did you like about this character?

_____

_____


BOOK TITLE: _____

AUTHOR: _____

FAVORITE CHARACTER: _____

FAVORITE SCENE: _____

What did you like about this character?

_____

_____


BOOK TITLE: _____

AUTHOR: _____

FAVORITE CHARACTER: _____

FAVORITE SCENE: _____

What did you like about this character?

_____

_____

# MORE BOOK FAVORITES:
## MOST TERRIFYING VILLAINS

BOOK TITLE: _____

AUTHOR: _____

FAVORITE CHARACTER: _____

FAVORITE SCENE: _____

What was so scary about this character?

_____

_____


BOOK TITLE: _____

AUTHOR: _____

FAVORITE CHARACTER: _____

FAVORITE SCENE: _____

What was so scary about this character?

_____

_____


BOOK TITLE: _____

AUTHOR: _____

FAVORITE CHARACTER: _____

FAVORITE SCENE: _____

What was so scary about this character?

_____

_____

## TODAY I . . . READ:

(LIST ALL OF THE THINGS YOU READ TODAY—
NEWSPAPERS, MAGAZINES, BOOKS, BLOGS, REVIEWS,
WORK- OR SCHOOL-RELATED TEXTS)

DATE: _____

1. _____

2. _____

3. _____

4. _____

5. _____

6. _____

7. _____

8. _____

9. _____

10. _____

11. _____

12. _____

13. _____

14. _____

15. _____

16. _____

# WHEN SOMEONE SAYS _____,
## YOU THINK . . .

Taboo:
_____

Tan:
_____

Tears:
_____

Tease:
_____

Theaters:
_____

Thunder:
_____

Ties:
_____

Time:
_____

Toll:
_____

Triumph:
_____

Truth:
_____

"This above all:
to thine own self be true."

—WILLIAM SHAKESPEARE,
*Hamlet*

# Right now I am thinking . . .

_____

_____

_____

_____

_____

_____

_____

_____

_____

# YOUR LISTS

Amusement park rides you have been on:

1. _____
2. _____
3. _____
4. _____
5. _____
6. _____
7. _____
8. _____


Businesses you'd like to start:

1. _____
2. _____
3. _____
4. _____
5. _____
6. _____
7. _____
8. _____

The best versions of a cover song:

1. _____

2. _____

3. _____

4. _____

5. _____

6. _____


The worst versions of a cover song:

1. _____

2. _____

3. _____

4. _____

5. _____

6. _____


Songs you would like to see covered, and by who:

1. _____

2. _____

3. _____

4. _____

5. _____

6. _____

**Things you like to do alone:**

1. _____
2. _____
3. _____
4. _____
5. _____
6. _____
7. _____
8. _____
9. _____
10. _____

**Things you prefer to do with other people:**

1. _____
2. _____
3. _____
4. _____
5. _____
6. _____
7. _____
8. _____
9. _____
10. _____

People whose journals you would like to read:

1. _____
2. _____
3. _____
4. _____
5. _____
6. _____
7. _____
8. _____
9. _____
10. _____

People you'd be willing to share this journal with:

1. _____
2. _____
3. _____
4. _____
5. _____
6. _____
7. _____
8. _____
9. _____
10. _____

# ASK SOMEONE

## THE NAME OF THE PERSON YOU'RE ASKING:

_____

In what part of the world do you imagine me being the happiest?

_____

What would you use to lure me into a trap?

_____

In a perfect world, who would I end up marrying?

_____

What is your favorite moment we've shared?

_____

What name do you think suits me better than my own?

_____

What things remind you of me?

_____

What do you hope I will always remember about you?

_____

# WHEN SOMEONE SAYS _____,
## YOU THINK . . .

Umbrellas:

_____

Unforgiving:

_____

Uniforms:

_____

Uptown:

_____

Urgent:

_____

Useful:

_____

Vacant:

_____

Vacuum:

_____

Vain:

_____

Vane:

_____

Violins:

_____

War:

_____

Waterfalls:

_____

Waves:

_____

Wheels:

_____

Whistles:

_____

Wind:

_____

Work:

_____

X-ray:

_____

Yoga:

_____

Youthful:

_____

Zest:

_____

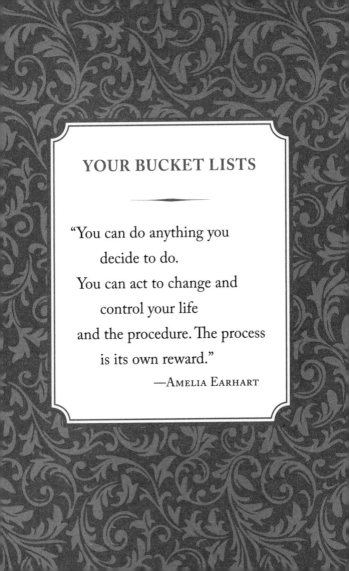

# YOUR BUCKET LISTS

"You can do anything you
decide to do.
You can act to change and
control your life
and the procedure. The process
is its own reward."

—AMELIA EARHART

# BUCKET LIST ITEMS

THINGS YOU WANT TO SOMEDAY DO OR LEARN,
THINGS YOU WANT TO SEE, OR PLACES YOU WANT TO
GO TO THAT START WITH THE LETTER

## A

1. _____

_____

2. _____

_____

3. _____

_____

4. _____

_____

5. _____

_____

6. _____

_____

7. _____

_____

8. _____

_____

# BUCKET LIST ITEMS

THINGS YOU WANT TO SOMEDAY DO OR LEARN,
THINGS YOU WANT TO SEE, OR PLACES YOU WANT TO
GO TO THAT START WITH THE LETTER

## C

1. _____

_____

2. _____

_____

3. _____

_____

4. _____

_____

5. _____

_____

6. _____

_____

7. _____

_____

8. _____

_____

# BUCKET LIST ITEMS

THINGS YOU WANT TO SOMEDAY DO OR LEARN,
THINGS YOU WANT TO SEE, OR PLACES YOU WANT TO
GO TO THAT START WITH THE LETTERS
**E** AND **F**

1. _____

_____

2. _____

_____

3. _____

_____

4. _____

_____

5. _____

_____

6. _____

_____

7. _____

_____

8. _____

_____

# BUCKET LIST ITEMS

THINGS YOU WANT TO SOMEDAY DO OR LEARN,
THINGS YOU WANT TO SEE, OR PLACES YOU WANT TO
GO TO THAT START WITH THE LETTER

## G

1. _____

_____

2. _____

_____

3. _____

_____

4. _____

_____

5. _____

_____

6. _____

_____

7. _____

_____

8. _____

_____

# BUCKET LIST ITEMS

THINGS YOU WANT TO SOMEDAY DO OR LEARN,
THINGS YOU WANT TO SEE, OR PLACES YOU WANT TO
GO TO THAT START WITH THE LETTER

**H**

1. _____

_____

2. _____

_____

3. _____

_____

4. _____

_____

5. _____

_____

6. _____

_____

7. _____

_____

8. _____

_____

# BUCKET LIST ITEMS

THINGS YOU WANT TO SOMEDAY DO OR LEARN,
THINGS YOU WANT TO SEE, OR PLACES YOU WANT TO
GO TO THAT START WITH THE LETTERS
**I** AND **J**

1. _____

   _____

2. _____

   _____

3. _____

   _____

4. _____

   _____

5. _____

   _____

6. _____

   _____

7. _____

   _____

8. _____

   _____

## BUCKET LIST ITEMS

THINGS YOU WANT TO SOMEDAY DO OR LEARN,
THINGS YOU WANT TO SEE, OR PLACES YOU WANT TO
GO TO THAT START WITH THE LETTER

**M**

1. _____
   _____

2. _____
   _____

3. _____
   _____

4. _____
   _____

5. _____
   _____

6. _____
   _____

7. _____
   _____

8. _____
   _____

# BUCKET LIST ITEMS

THINGS YOU WANT TO SOMEDAY DO OR LEARN,
THINGS YOU WANT TO SEE, OR PLACES YOU WANT TO
GO TO THAT START WITH THE LETTERS
**N** AND **O**

1. _____
_____

2. _____
_____

3. _____
_____

4. _____
_____

5. _____
_____

6. _____
_____

7. _____
_____

8. _____
_____

# BUCKET LIST ITEMS

THINGS YOU WANT TO SOMEDAY DO OR LEARN,
THINGS YOU WANT TO SEE, OR PLACES YOU WANT TO
GO TO THAT START WITH THE LETTERS
**Q** AND **R**

1. _____

    _____

2. _____

    _____

3. _____

    _____

4. _____

    _____

5. _____

    _____

6. _____

    _____

7. _____

    _____

8. _____

    _____

# BUCKET LIST ITEMS

THINGS YOU WANT TO SOMEDAY DO OR LEARN,
THINGS YOU WANT TO SEE, OR PLACES YOU WANT TO
GO TO THAT START WITH THE LETTER

**T**

1. _____

    _____

2. _____

    _____

3. _____

    _____

4. _____

    _____

5. _____

    _____

6. _____

    _____

7. _____

    _____

8. _____

    _____

# BUCKET LIST ITEMS

THINGS YOU WANT TO SOMEDAY DO OR LEARN,
THINGS YOU WANT TO SEE, OR PLACES YOU WANT TO
GO TO THAT START WITH THE LETTERS
**U** AND **V**

1. _____

_____

2. _____

_____

3. _____

_____

4. _____

_____

5. _____

_____

6. _____

_____

7. _____

_____

8. _____

_____

# BUCKET LIST ITEMS

THINGS YOU WANT TO SOMEDAY DO OR LEARN,
THINGS YOU WANT TO SEE, OR PLACES YOU WANT TO
GO TO THAT START WITH THE LETTERS
**X** AND **Y** AND **Z**

1. _____

   _____

2. _____

   _____

3. _____

   _____

4. _____

   _____

5. _____

   _____

6. _____

   _____

7. _____

   _____

8. _____

   _____

"To accomplish great things
we must not only act,
but also dream;
not only plan, but also believe.
—ANATOLE FRANCE

# NOTES

# NOTES

NOTES

Project editor/additional text:
Barbara Berger, Sterling Publishing

Original design:
Christine Heun, Sterling Publishing

## ABOUT THE AUTHOR

**Shane Windham** is the author of more than 30 books, an independent recording artist, and the designer of numerous unique table games. He lives in northeast Texas, and maintains a strong presence on social media.

**www.shanewindham.com**

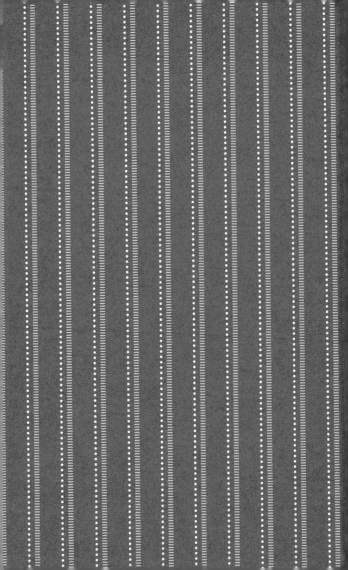